Helping Children Grieve Through Sacred Actions and Images

Michelle Ryan, MA

As You Wish Publishing, LLC
Connect@asyouwishpublishing.com

ISBN-13: 978-1-951131-06-7

Library of Congress Control Number: 2020914955
Cover Illustration by Molly Ryan, MFA
Photo of Author by Julie Ulstrup Photography Studio

Printed in the United States of America.

Nothing in this book or any affiliations with this book is a
substitute for medical or psychological help. If you are
needing help please seek it.

Dedication

To my family and teachers who have expressed so much
love, patience, and faith in me until I could.
To all the children who allowed me to learn and love them.

The moose shines her light on this path. The cow leads the way while watching her child. Loving strength in her care for the children, acknowledging a job well done.

Table of Contents

Introduction

My own experience is the material for this book. While I have collected data as a special education teacher and analyzed the data to create Individual Education Plans during my career, the stories, strategies, and techniques in this book, I collected through my own experience of living through grief and supporting children. Some of the methods may be research-based; however, I am not presenting them in this context as scientific or proven with research backing my premise. I have experienced considerable support for myself and children I worked with and loved through using these strategies to the point I felt compelled to share them with other parents, grandparents, teachers, hospice workers, and all adults close to children.

I base this book on my experience being present with my feelings following loss in my life. I have used all the strategies described. I have practiced sacred acts and still do to this day to honor my love and experiences.

I thank all my teachers, family, friends, mentors, therapists, and helpers who supported me along this journey of accepting loss, accepting painful feelings, accepting what I cannot change and being loving to myself. You see, my mother died when she was young. For me, that was not a desire as a young mother. I became a seeker, a conscious seeker, with many resources and support to heal, to live fully. Today, many years later, I am still seeking and learning the terrain through feelings of grief, love, sadness, fear, and love and loss.

I stand on many shoulders of helpers I have had along the way with so much creativity and artistry. I flow in the river of feelings with greater ease and skill to hold those I love dearly in their streams of emotions. I frequently walk, run, and travel to the grieving tent. To the messy experience of heart-wrenching love through sacred actions to all that comfort, clarify, hold, and flow the truth of love and loss. I hope to share these stories guiding us to fully expressing our humanity.

I hope in this book to share some of what has helped me along the way. To make transparent what actions have helped my children, grandchildren, and students in special education survive and face the process of their feelings thoroughly—having to find ground after a loss. To help children find softness and truth following first losses, the steps to connect to our human universal and individual resources, to find healing and liveability, sacred actions, and spiritual faith.

Foreword

In the summer of 2019, six months before there was ever mention of the coronavirus, I was collecting pink sea shells on a beach in Florida with a friend. I was hoping to get a glimpse of the playful way a dolphin moves from the depths of the water up to the surface. My friend was taking a break from writing this book to love me exactly where I was.

There are special people in life that are capable of offering that type of love. Take a moment to see if any of them come to your mind. If you have not had this experience of love yet, it is my pleasure to introduce you to Michelle Ryan. Michelle teaches, speaks, and connects to others from the place of love. For years, long before we ever became friends, I watched her facilitate healing and show up reliably for others in her life. Michelle's reliability stems from the choice to be a loving observer of life. This tenderness supports the generations in her family, her students, and her friends. Her love creates a boundary in which others can explore the depths of human emotions.

Michelle's book, *Helping Children Grieve Through Sacred Actions and Images*, artfully shares stories of resiliency that are volunteered from her own life on how to create these boundaries, like the grieving tent that she designed on her farm, to give grief a space in her life. This book is a guide for those who want to join the sacred circle of helpers.

The format of this book offers layers of healing by exploring the transitory aspects of everyday life. These potent stories offer credible images of how resiliency can be built through practicing during the hardest parts. Michelle creates an accessible path to facilitate multi-generational support in the family system. As a special education teacher, she gently shares how to guide a student touched by loss to begin to experience their agency in the educational system. She even playfully expresses dissatis-faction with sacred tantrums.

If you only get one message from this book, I hope you learn that our "grief is as deep as the love." We will continue to experience grief. There is always loss. Grief doesn't tell time. Think of the collective loss that we continue to experience in our world. Grief means that you love. Sometimes we have to let go of the people we love too soon. We have the choice to hold onto the love we shared with them.

On that hot summer day in 2019, on a beach in Florida, we were having so much fun that we forgot to stop for lunch or take refuge from the sun. I felt like an eight-year-old again playing on my childhood beach on Long Island. The act of playing is such a crucial piece of how children learn skills that allow them to step into adulthood whole. Feelings cannot be experienced selectively. Children may be unable to connect to the jubilant parts of life if they disconnect from their feelings of grief. It is your job to learn how to love them exactly as they are until they can accept that love inside of themselves. *Helping Children Grieve* presents a unique opportunity for you to learn the skills necessary to take on this task.

As the sun started to set that day, a dolphin began joyously swimming in the crests of the waves where the sand met the ocean. That is my hope for how you implement this book in your life. Utilize this book as a tool to support children so they can safely dive into the depths of their emotions and take the time to come up for air to roll into the waves of life playfully.

Your Fellow Change Agent,

Kate Cash

Chapter

One

Sacred Actions For Myself

I have a personal relationship with activating sacred actions for myself to keep memories and love alive. I find that tending to these relationships of loss with concrete gestures in my surroundings serve several support purposes for me. First, I acknowledge and honor the loss and love I have. Second, this action gives movement to my feelings, so they have a place and do not remain inside of me, causing build-up, stuckness, and lack of expression. Third, I am taking the time to honor my loss. Fourth, the actions usually take a creative form or relationship form, such as decor in my home, a piece of spirit artwork, or serving another human being with what I have learned from my love and loss with intention. Fifth, the outcome is I have a positive reminder and place to breathe and say yes to my love and loss. These actions heal me. These actions give expression to my grief. These actions give voice from me to the universe that this person and their passing has touched me. These actions are a communication to the beloved of spirit and the treasure I loved and who loved me. These actions fill the hole that the loss has created. These actions allow life to continue through me. These actions are sacred tending.

Here is an example. When my first husband and I were separating, we lived in two different states. My young daughters went to spend Christmas with their father, which was the right thing to do yet heartbreaking. Yes, heartbreaking to me. I thought the only reason to do holiday traditions was for the children, and since they were gone, I would not. I was frozen and devastated about the ending of our family as I had hoped, expected, and known it to be. I created many expectations from my images, beliefs, and values; of what a whole, a good family form was during my life. Now I had many unmet expectations, self-judgments, disappointments, and grief.

My wise, caring teacher was continually checking on me and noticed. He suggested I get a Christmas tree. I argued with him it would be too emotional. After a while, I listened. I was so uncomfortable, and what did I have to lose? It would keep me moving if nothing else, satisfy him, and I could at least report I had done as he suggested when I complained.

I went to the grocery and found a small evergreen. I was also to gather some ribbon. I love being around color! I picked two rolls: one sparkly red and another glittering purple. When I brought the tree home, I watered the tree and sat and smelled the tree. I was already coming out of my funk, my helplessness. The pause was different than the frozenness I was experiencing before. I just sat with this sacred action for a while. Taking in the power I was feeling.

When I was ready for the next step, I lined the tree with white angel lights. Feeling my daughters and all they gave me in spirit and love. Motherhood is a sacred experience of a depth I still marvel. The instructions had been to take the ribbon and tie bows on the tree, saying a prayer with each tie. I tenderly began, feeling a little embarrassed at first, then remembering my mother and grandmother showing me how to light the candles in worship at the Cathedral altar. With each bow, my strength and faith grew. My self-esteem improved, and negative self-talk and concerns abated for moments. I felt seen, and this action felt right to me as well. My teacher knew me well. I began to smile, cry, and own my life. My soul mattered in this holy time of year. Realizing I participated in my own life. I sent prayers to my children with gratitude. I said prayers of tears to the pain of the present and past. I grew lighter.

This foundational moment in owning my life and shifting how I grieved changed me. Potent learning occurred over the week of that first Christmas without my daughters. I was able to ease into being alone and enjoy a few moments of freedom and rest. Each year as the children visited their father, it was hard in the anticipation and reality of their leaving, yet I knew how to survive and maybe thrive while they lived their time with their father.

Many years later, I created another tree to honor the passing of my first mother-in-law before the holidays. She was and is a treasure to me, my daughters, and her whole family. She uniquely saw me, and I will always be grateful to her. Her passing created many holes and requirements in our family. I had to do a lot of my grieving on my own since I was divorced from her son. Being divorced brought many hardships to the grieving process for me. What she meant to her granddaughters and me and all the love and support she expressed over her life was profound. With the aid of the sacred container of therapy, my therapist and I revealed the way spirit spoke to me, how to keep her spirit alive, and grow myself as a mother and matriarch. This woman embraced my love of everything *pink*. She and her husband planted hundreds of pink geraniums around their front yard as a welcome path in 1984 for our July wedding held in their backyard. Over the years, she continued to show me her love and support me through the actions of pink. She always permitted me to express in pink; never saying enough is enough. While sitting in the therapist's office, I saw the image of a small, white Christmas tree with white lights. Remembering the glass ornaments I had bought in St. Louis the first Christmas preparing for my eldest daughter's birth and pink satin bows that were in a storage box at home. Rosette clips were part of the package. Strings of pink beads and white beads completed my pink tree decor from the '80s. I haven't hung these decorations on the tree in years but still loved them. I knew I needed to bring these beauties out of the basement into the light of my yoga meditation room and adore my beloved first mother figure after the death of my mother.

My heart softens with the plan, a purpose. The tree is still up in my sacred space. Even today, it is reminding me to write this piece. I have changed the ornamentals throughout the 18 months since her death. I am continuing to have a daily connection, beauty, and support.

This collection of stories is my sacred action for the children and the young experience of loss in each of us.

With love,

Michelle

Chapter

Two

Grief is as Deep as the Love

This statement can be as true and deep as our capacity to be present, to feel our hearts and be with ourselves and each other. Grief has been a frequent visitor in my life. As I researched my lineage and found plenty in my ancestry of the Irish, people with mental health challenges and facing repression hardships were present. I lost my mother when she was 40 years old in the spring of my senior year of high school. The shock of her death and this loss has guided me to this point of having the experience to share. I have learned how to utilize this unfortunate reality as a resource, and I feel I have used it well to help others. Many have asked me to share my wisdom around connecting with children, especially children who have had a loss or trauma.

As adults, we need to do our own work when helping children. Learn our own inner landscape. Have enough experience with our own feelings and pathways to know the road in and out with our own meanings and feelings to guide children in this terrain. While traveling with children, do not be surprised if your own path and landscape become vaster. This is the power of working with children following loss and trauma. The healing potential grows as we witness and hold children in their expressions and take the time to honor their own experiences following deep moments of connection with a child in sadness.

Another consideration, for our own awareness, the deeper and more accepting we are with the rainbow of feelings and experiences within our own selves, the more available we are to the children in need in our life. The more we can allow our feelings in our personal growth, the more we can allow the child safe holding during feeling all they need to feel. Our ability to give permission to all that is within ourselves, we can give permission for the feeling to be lived in our children.

The calmer and more secure as a feeling person we are, we can maintain connection to ourselves, the child in the present moment, and move with the movement of feelings. Our histories become information to inform us without taking over the moments with the child.

Having deep kinesthetic experiences within our spectrum of feelings allows us to guide from this knowledge of wisdom and safety.

If we have experienced the pendulum ourselves, we can predict and know this too shall pass. We can use the grief cycle as a map that may veer off to the left or right or speed up or slow down but will arrive for a pause sooner than later.

I highly suggest we, as adults, model these ways of living our feelings and seek our own safety net of a sacred circle of helpers to guide and witness our own sacred actions.

"We get together on the basis of our similarities; we grow on the basis of our differences." Virginia Satir

Chapter

Three

Positive Intention

Base of All Actions

I taught and parented from the perspective of the positive intention coined by the world-renowned leader Virginia Satir. She traveled the world in the 1970s and 1980s watching how families communicate. Noticing five basic similarities in human communications, she documented her observations in her book, *Peoplemaking*. She wrote the books, *Self Esteem, Making Contact, Your Many Faces* and *The Satir Model*. Virginia Satir was a social worker and leading humanitarian. I learned of her work through her books and her students who attended her month-long intensives in Crested Butte, Colorado. My primary teacher in this model of healing has been Steven Young, the founder and trainer for Peoplemaking of Colorado and Teacher of the Human Validation Process Model. All this to explain the origins and how I learned of the positive intention that aligned with my core beliefs.

*The Positive Intention Model acknowledges that we all wake each morning to do the best we can with our lives. We have human yearnings to experience ourselves as loving, able to take risks, be generative, and to have a choice. Positive Intention refers to our attempts to live as best we can to meet these universal human yearnings within ourselves. Our behaviors come from this place of the positive intention to make our own lives better. Sometimes our strategies do not match well or are in our best interest to live our yearnings fully. Now the strategies may not be the best in obtaining these goals, so feedback and loving education are helpful to fine-tune our actions, but at the core, remembering the positive intention takes the sting out of the motive piece of behavior. If we as adults see all children's behaviors as a call for help, a call for expression, a call to be heard, we can show up in a way that supports the children's expression and learning.

My goal is to support children in finding behaviors that lead to more fulfillment of their universal yearnings that all humans have and that fit well into our social constructs. I teach a variety of choices in behaviors to match the different relationships we as humans engage in society so that realization of yearnings and social norms can be honored with the awareness of the varieties of cultural images, values, and beliefs we carry as well. Recognizing we have a choice in our own experience through our inner landscape and, therefore, can respond to life is a maturity piece that trauma and loss can interfere with; the human maturity of being the choice makers in our own life. As a teacher, I slow the process down so that a student can think about and experience more possibilities.

I see all behaviors of children as communication. They may not know the words or be able to regulate their emotions or understand themselves or the world; however, they learn through acting out and how the world responds to them. That is why adults in children's lives are important teachers and need to see children as learners. We all do better when we know better.

"Do the best you can until you know better. Then when you know better, do better." Maya Angelou

Virginia Satir communicated this idea in her work beginning in the 60s with her beliefs about everyone being good at their core, and their coping skills were ultimately what led to surface issues. She added that all people are capable of change, and therefore focusing on the skills will lead people towards living their fullest lives. She saw the potential in all people.

I find the element of taking a no-judgment-based response to children's behaviors frees up space to respond and be curious about the behavior and to problem solve without blame. The child is given permission to investigate and change without loss of dignity or esteem. When I come towards a child's behavior in judgment, this closes the options of response and creates a punishment response. I ascertain we do not want to punish natural human response to pain and suffering, and I offer we want to aid in the healing and feeling of these natural feelings through safe and honorable behavior by the adults as well as children. I find assuming the positive intention to do better, to learn and express appropriately and move on with living beneficially to my overall goal of self-respect for all, especially children. I find living from this belief in the positive intention supports the creative process of sacred action of healing and feeling.

Many times, I pause when agitated with a child expressing anger and hurt and I ask myself, what is the child saying? What do they want and need? What is the underlying communication they are saying through dumping all the pencils on the floor, knocking over a desk, and running out of the classroom? Instead of coming from seeing the child as "bad," for not following the rules of social engagement in school, the behavior is an opportunity to investigate and solve. This does not mean that the child is not required to do a do-over and be responsible for their actions. It just means I wait for when the child is available for learning and can regulate their feelings before expecting account-ability.

I expect the child to be doing the best they can at this moment until they can do better, over and over, until that magical moment when the child says, "I am angry. Help."

Or when the student turns a card over on their desk that signals, "My feelings are too big for me" and "I am going to my safe space." All of the increments of teaching and allowing, the patience and mistakes to come to the moment of integration and ability for the student to be self-aware and take care of oneself during big feelings begin with the initial permission to welcome all feelings and behaviors as the road to learning, as part of learning, and belonging here with the child.

"Everything everyone does, is their way to make their lives better, whether it looks that way or not." Steven Young

*Young, Steven (1994), Human Validation Process Model, Class 1 & 2.

Chapter
Four

Jacob's Story

Grief Healing in a Public School

In 2010, I was working as a special education resource teacher in an elementary school, in addition to being a parent and grandparent. Having returned to public school teaching after several years as a private tutor, this was my second year at this school, and I had a tremendous longing to serve the community in a humanistic manner. I felt I had natural and unique skills to bring to the school environment.

Our special education team met weekly to discuss needs on our caseloads and within the school in general, as well as scheduling and professional development. Our school had another group of general education teachers who discussed student needs and interventions weekly, which members from the special education team attended. One little boy was being seen by our social worker and known in the school for two years since his mother died while he was a kindergarten student. Since I was relatively new to the school, and he was not popping up during his first-grade year, I had not heard or met him yet or began tracking him.

As his behaviors began to escalate during second grade, he became a more significant concern for his teachers. Jacob was being less responsive to intervention, and his teacher brought him to my attention. Due to the structure of the special education team, I would not have been the case manager by the organization. Several factors changed how I became his teacher. I mention this because I found these factors paramount to how we serve children. Many times helping a child requires listening to the vocational and universal call, whether it fits in the referral process or not. The resources Jacob needed around the grief I had. I felt the purpose and gratitude for his pain. I felt a duty to say 'yes' to his needs.

Jacob had lost his mother at a young age; his single father was doing the best he could and asked for help. The other teachers and students in the community did not have personal experience with this type of loss. This child and his loss spoke to me directly. Of course, he was having tantrums and running from class and school. He needed individual support around this loss and his feelings. He missed having care each morning to get ready for school. He woke himself up each day and went to school on his own while his Dad was at work.

I knew he was mine. That was how the gift of surviving and thriving after losing my mother would serve this child. I knew the experience of being that teenager whose mother had killed herself as I walked the halls of high school, seeing the sympathy in the teachers' eyes, yet knowing they did not know what to do or say further isolated me. My dad was toughing it out and doing his best, just like this child's father. I was the kid who felt ashamed, lost, and scared and expressed it through anger, depression, and destructive behaviors. I stepped in to support and serve this child and stepped up to the relief of my coworkers. I worked through my relationships with all my students. I was given more leeway with this child since there was relief among the staff that he was receiving extra services.

As the universe would have it, our relationship started during one of his runs from class. The following day after the intervention team decided for me to look into the situation, the social worker was with him in the hall near my classroom. We had his father's permission for me to build a relationship with him and to see where it would go. Before I had the chance for a proactive introduction with this boy, as often happens in a busy school, the office called me to go out to the hall to support the social worker. I was meeting him in crisis. I could hear the anger and pain expressed by him. I walked out to the hallway and asked the social worker if I could be of help so the boy could hear. I started by just sitting near him on the floor. I offered to help and told him I would listen to his complaints. He was hiding his face and body as best he could in the corner of a narrow hallway. I felt the pain in his body as he rolled himself into a ball. I breathed and waited. I spoke to him through the social worker, an adult he knew.

We met this way. By validating his feelings and giving him choices, he agreed to come to my classroom, which was near, for a snack. Having a snack would be the beginning of one of the primary ways of sacred actions I would take with him and teach him self care and caring for his feelings. Addressing his mandala of care and connection, we as a pair and a team identified his needs and found ways that fit in his family, culture, and the school environment to meet these needs. The Self Mandala, as documented in *The New*

Peoplemaking on pages 43-50, includes the needs of humans to thrive, starting at the center with basic physical needs and circles out. Maslow's Hierarchy of Needs identified these needs as well. Using these models and my own experience with self mandala development enhancement, I nurtured Jacob in his environment. I taught him how to do so for himself over the four years of our teacher/student relationship.

THE SELF MANDALA

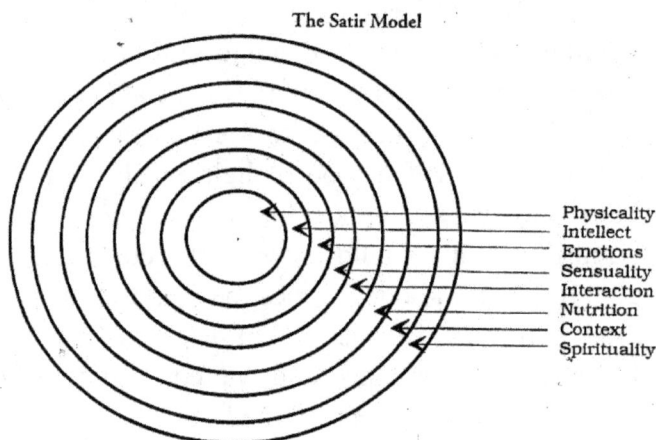

The Satir Model

Physicality
Intellect
Emotions
Sensuality
Interaction
Nutrition
Context
Spirituality

In *The New Peoplemaking*, Satir wrote her description of developing health for ourselves. I followed and engaged these ideas in my Individual Education Plan for Jacob and taught him transparently along the way what I saw he needed, enjoyed and responded to, to help grow his capacity to cope with living his life as it was positively and what he could change and how to change.

Here is Satir's teaching:

"As we increase our knowledge of ourselves, developing and maintaining health becomes paramount. To create the best possible scenario for our total health and well-being, we would:

Give our body good care, attention, exercise, and love.

Develop our intellect through learning how we learn and surround ourselves with stimulating ideas, books, activities, learning experiences, and opportunities to engage in dialogue with others.

Give ourselves permission to become friendly with our feelings that they work for us instead of against us.

Develop our senses, learn about their care, and think of them and use them as vital avenues to bring things into ourselves.

Develop harmonious ways of problem-solving, nurturing, and conflict resolution; and develop congruent and healthy relationships.

Learn what nutritional needs are and provide for them, remembering that each person's body is unique. Eating strawberries gives one person hives; another will have a tasty treat.

Provide the place where you live and work with the kinds of sights, sounds, temperature, light, color, quality of air, and space that more fully support life.

Engage yourself with what it means to be alive, to be a part of the universe, to fully manifest yourself, and to know that there is a life force outside yourself."

I agree and base so much of my life and teachings on these tenets. Virginia's book was copyrighted in 1988. I suspect if she and I could have a conversation today, we would discuss her statement, "There is a life force outside yourself." I have come to believe and experience myself as part of the life force within me. I would love to discuss with her the depth of her meaning and experience on this topic.

The mandala is especially helpful in understanding and helping students with special needs. Assimilation of the mandala with the need to utilize students' strengths and to support their challenges create robust Individual Education Plans. This list became my foundation for helping parents and students to live more fully themselves through their experiences in learning and with the school. I will describe examples through this story and others where you may notice these needs addressed. The first seven areas in the mandala were very applicable to the school environments. Number eight, spiritual engagement is very personal. I am sharing my beliefs here, even in the title of my book. Now that I am in the private sector, I feel free to do so, and those who are attracted can pick up and receive as they choose. While in public school, I kept my beliefs private out of respect for the separation stated in our constitution, to be professional, and respect for all views.

The school environment and children were a perfect petri dish for me to grow my understanding of my mandala, and my spiritual beliefs grew and sustained me.

Personalizing

With Jacob, I analyzed his family structure with the mandala and used my emotional landscape as a child with a sick mother that I had interpreted for myself. Mothers and others who take on the primary role of care for a child tend to their basic needs of food, clothing, home, comfort, and validation of feelings of who they are. This parent holds big emotions for the small child. This primary caregiver tends to the child's mandala. This boy had lost his mother to addiction and death at a young age. In many ways, he had an immature developmental response to life in an eight-year-old body with older responsibilities for himself he had to utilize in his home environment. The conflict was hard for him in many ways and showed up as rebellion, aggression, tantrums, and loss of control of his feelings and body. He did not fit in the hierarchy of the school since he had to be self-reliant. He did not have the skills to process his feelings. He needed safety to change his experience in life and at school.

From the first meeting, Jacob clearly stated he was the only one who did not have a mom, and no one knew how he felt. He was so furious when he told me this belief.

I used my yogic breath, mirroring him, sitting in a small chair at a small table, so our eyes were level, and our hearts were level, and I met him from person to person. "I lost my mom when I was a child," I told him softly. "We never know what others have experienced unless we talk about it."

His interest peaked. I had gained some influence with him around "mom death." I was also an example of someone who had survived my mother dying. I was a person of authority who was showing vulnerability and success with this situation of no mother. I was teaching a possibility he had not known because he did not know anyone else who had lost their mother.

I breathed and connected to myself; I sat near him and witnessed Jacob first before any other action. I related to him through my breath and eyes, ears, and heart. I connected to the context of his family and in the school. From there, a container was established for us to problem solve and build trust.

It was helpful that I had a similar wound and powerful for easing Jacob and me into a trusting relationship. However, the same trauma was not required. As long as adults and professionals in children's lives we proceed from the "sameness" belief that all people are more alike than different and faced with pain and suffering or loss, in this case, we will respond similarly. Sameness theory is another teaching from the Human Validation Process Model. We all know of loss from a very young age. Living includes loss. It is going to happen; as long as we love, we will lose. So while I used the information of my personal story, I connected with other children with breath and validation even when the life experience differed. We can find physical connection, sameness, empathy, and humanity through the shared experiences of love and loss, of wanting to belong, wanting to create, wanting to have a choice, and being willing to take a risk. Being inclined to be vulnerable and real is a choice we all have as humans and helpers. My experience is that I have to be willing to be authentic to be a long-lasting support to a child. They, in turn, heal and internalize a new understanding around validation of themselves to grow and learn.

I was listening to him. I was feeding him literally and figuratively. In the Hierarchy of Needs Model, this child was physically hungry and emotionally hungry. Students can not be available for learning when their basic needs are not met. I began my work with him by showing I noticed his needs. We named his needs, and we met his needs. I told him with my actions and words, I will do this for you because I care, and you need it, and over time, you will learn and be able to do so for yourself. The academic setting was beyond his reach as long as he was in survival mode. As professionals, we need to acknowledge students' physical and emotional needs have value for our work in academic environments to reach the children. There are times the child's actual academic learning is to learn emotional equilibrium. Learning emotional capabilities must be genuinely honored as an academic job for this student to proceed and gain their academic achievements. These holes in the child's development need to be filled for progress to be made. As this child will show us when tended to many times, the student will catch up academically.

Now, I am fully aware of the overburden put on our teachers in the schools at this time in our public institute-ions. I am very grateful for the support and generosity allowed me as a resource teacher, and this child to do the work needed in this school. It was because of the very dedicated work of all the adults of this school showing up for this child: his father, the principal, classroom teachers, male teachers as role models, secretaries, special-ists, janitors, and other students and their parents this child grew. I will give examples of how each within their roles and humanity showed up. But I must say our Federal, State, and District Organizations, struggle to maintain resources in schools for this essential and said required work. For our children to be available and achieve high expectations, our society set for students to graduate and be contributing members. Yet too many times, these human resources are stretched to the breaking point by policy and budget decisions separated from these human needs for the student and teacher to thrive.

Flexibility and Crisis Plan

As I reviewed Jacob's behavior record and his teachers' concerns, the first behaviors to address were tantrums in the classroom and running. It was going to take some trial and error to document his triggers and until we had some predictive abilities to his stressors. I set up my classes to be covered by my co-worker if crisis calls came from Jacob's teachers. At this time, he could not settle his outburst on his own or in the classroom. The goal was to respond to the disturbances in a new way with the safety of my class for him before we could move towards preventing eruptions. After a couple more episodes of pencil throwing and table-turning, we were able to get him to use a signal system to let his teacher know his feelings were getting too big to manage, and he was going to Ms. Ryan's room. This way allowed more safety and serenity in the classroom, and he could leave the stressful environment with permission and control, thus changing the running behavior, which was unsafe and disruptive to all. All the participants were learning to trust the boy's urgency and safety plan. He was learning to notice his feelings and some choices around feelings. He was also learning the identification of emotions and a slight pause to his actions.

Schools' survival is based on structure. It is a tall order to ask the adults to trust students' movements and allow the teachers to empower a child to be different. Yet in this example, the child was already disrupting the order whenever, wherever, so what was there to lose? I reassured my colleagues that while it may get worse before better, I believed and had experienced that humans want to belong, and as he felt safer and more in charge of himself, as we meet these needs in him, his disruptive behaviors would lessen. My specialized education training has included work in a therapeutic school program with a triad of services between mental health, social services, and special education in a day program. I have seen significant changes in children suffering from all sorts of neglect and abuse and trusted these methods. Meet the children where they are and give them safe choices.

Jacob had a laminated card in his desk that he placed on top of his desk that said "Ms. Ryan's Room." His teacher would call me so I would make sure he got to my room. While we were teaching him this signal system, he ran a few more times, but he soon used the system as we hoped. In these last few runs, the principal, 4th-grade teacher, and gym teacher would all be helpful and available to be calm, firm, and safe guides to get Jacob to the resource room, to process the stressful events and equilibrate. Jacob started trusting that we had his back, and while he would be required to acknowledge his disruptions and make amends, he was not in "trouble," and his concerns were taken seriously. He began to use the card and left the classroom without an alarm to the whole system. These were Jacob's first successes.

While Jacob settled in his classroom with his classroom teacher, he continued with some outbursts in other environments: the playground and music class. The strategy to support him and maintain safety for other children was to have another adult on the playground who was watching and observing his interactions. The adults intervene in stressful moments and proactively to promote positive play and support all the children in confident problem-solving skills. Having eyes and ears on Jacob and other children helped our assessments and learning his triggers and needs, as well as supporting many interactions on the playground to calm, safe learning conclusions instead of big emotional contact problems resulting in disciplinary actions. Playground duty was always one of my favorite ways to get to know children and contribute to developing social skills such as friendship building and maintenance. Many reputation repairs happened in those early days. We decreased Jacob's conflicts and changed other children being afraid of him. He was very athletic, so otherwise found the playground an area he excelled in.

The music class took some more in-depth conversations. The music teacher reported him saying mean comments to other children, a concern of his treatment of instruments, and lack of following directions leading to outburst. That first meeting we had in the hall was outside the music room following an outburst and run from music class. We first put another adult in class to support the music teacher if he acted out. The music teacher and I each had some one-on-one conversations with him. The music teacher expressed her desire to have him in class and how she saw his talent in all music activities each time she spoke to him and me. With the social worker, he was able to work out that the music reminded him of his mother. He did not like to think of her. It hurt, and that made him mad. Processing these feelings in private helped his understanding of what was happening "to him." From there, we were able to create some strategies, support from him when he felt these feelings in music and then some choices. First, he was allowed the big feelings' pass. Soon he and his music teacher preferred he not leave class or outburst because music class time was so limited. Secondly, he was allowed to bring his instrument to my classroom so he could work through frustrations in privacy and have more ease in the group setting. Another empowerment strategy, he made a list of activities that he found stressful in music that reminded him of his mom and shared this list with the music teacher with my support. The teacher would proactively let him know when he came to class if one of those activities would be in the lesson of the day. That way, he would be ready and not surprised during the stress of music. She was creating awareness and choices for him, which lessened the pressure on Jacob's school day.

Nourishment, Mothering and Community, Building and Artistic Expression

Once Jacob was in my room, following big emotions, I would feed him first. I would not try to talk to him. We had documented that most outbursts were times when he was likely hungry. He told me he was hungry each time I saw him leading to me incorporating food into his service plan. I made sure I met him each morning for a hello and snack. Remember, he was on his own in the morning. He did not have an adult at home to wish him a good day and make sure he ate before leaving for school. His foundation of care was lacking and needed attention. I wanted him to know someone was there for him. This quick touching base on the playground or in his classroom during planner time went far in proactively supporting him and lessening his outburst. By feeding him, he was less likely to get over-hungry. We were addressing one of the precipitating factors: hunger. Also, a pat on the back, I am here for you, someone is here for you, and I see you. "Good Morning." Using his mandala as our guide to his nutrition and his emotions, relational, and interaction circles were being influenced positively at school.

He and his teachers brought to my attention that during field trips, he did not have lunch. Our school district did provide sack lunches for children on free and reduced lunch programs. When I went to the lady who served lunch and asked her for lunch for him for a Friday field trip, she smiled. She knew Jacob and felt and cared for him. She was happy he was looked after and glad to make his lunch and be part of his team. She increased her special welcome each day during lunch service. Also, I increased my connections within the building. As I worked with Jacob's needs, I received many benefits as well as increasing my confidence in the sameness principles and pillars of healthy mandala for humans. Taking risks to ask for help on

Jacob's behalf, I grew my interactional circle at school and broadened both of our social networks. I could have easily made lunch for him myself, which I have done many times with other students. I was attentive this time to establishing a resilient, robust community response for this student and increasing the program of individual education resources and allies.

Jacob had his spot in my room; a table with supplies for him: colored pencils, his journal, fidget/touching objects, and magnet puzzle toy that he liked. He could eat his snack and lower his overwhelm before I processed what happened with him and why he was in my room. When a person, especially a child with trauma, is upset, asking questions of them continues the overstimulation to their system. I would either make eye contact and a nod or walk by with a light touch to signal I knew he was there and allowed him to calm down. Nonverbal communication was vital to him, and he responded well to my body language, and I was aware of his. Again, very similar to the primary bond language of care a mother gives, and he was missing. I tended to his need for physical touch and comfort when he allowed for this physicality with pats on the back and side hugs.

Jacob was an intelligent, artistic kid. Having art supplies at his spot gave him a way to use his hands and release the tension he was experiencing, so I had these supplies available. Sometimes if I didn't have other students in the room, I would sit with him and draw and color as a way to connect and model for him. My participation legitimized the strategies I was showing him as useful and essential to my life and emotional equilibrium as well.

Problem Solving

As he calmed and when I had the time to give, we worked on figuring out the problem. What had happened that he had gotten mad? Mad was his primary feeling for the first several months I worked with him. He was mad that his life was different than the other kids, mad at his dad, mad that his mom was gone mad, Mad, MAD! I knew mad covered up sadness, and we needed to allow the mad in healthy ways before sadness could show its vulnerable underbelly. I accepted all he revealed to me and validated as best I could. I continued to normalize his experience with stories of my life. Sometimes other kids in the classroom could normalize with their mad and sad stories. Additional children can be so supportive in a milieu of this kind. All the kids in my class had their struggles to accept and deal with, and they were very generous in sharing and support-ing each other at whatever level they were available.

What happened? Asking him what he saw and heard. What was the activity? What did that mean when? How did you feel? All these questions establish the conditions for him experiencing a problem at this time. We noticed it was often during writing time that he would have a problem. His high emotional alert from the grief and self-reliance were stressing the task of writing. His frustration with writing being a hard activity for him was harder than his system could process. Writing requires a connection to self and self-awareness that children in pain are often avoiding, making writing near impossible until dealing with the self. Writing is communication, and if there is a resistance or block in communicating, writing can be a problem area.

After some assessment, the decision was made that his academic service time would be with writing assignments.

Jacob often upset the classroom, his teachers, and other students. He carried a heavy burden of his "bad" behaviors when he was upset, increasing his stress. We created a "do-over" policy. As he calmed down and addressed his feelings, he then considered how this affected others. If he was sorry, ashamed, embarrassed, or guilty—no problem. These feelings meant he cared. We all let expression happen, and we learn and apologize. How will we do it differently next time? He came up with how he could do it better when mad in the future, when disappointed in the future, when all the ways life and school were unfair. We have choices, and when we have opportunities to learn and try again. Jacob became comfortable with owning his mistakes, trying a new behavior, and apologizing. We would role-play in my room possible stressors and redo's together. I would support him in his return to class and redo.

Scheduling

The support of the school personnel was so phenomenal in these situations. I was able to establish weekly one-on-one writing instruction with Jacob to work on his writing skills as well as using this as a safe, proactive instruction time around feeling and social-emotional education. The goal was to integrate the grade-level writing curriculum and instruction with his emotional needs. Having the one on one was a luxury in the public school day and week, yet so crucial for the privacy and depth of the work required to move Jacob from survival to coping to thriving. I brought in emotional education books to support our discussions, and we would discuss and write responses to what we read. In the beginning, I scribed for him, and he illustrated. I scribed for him to give him a distant expression to the intense feelings that he was not familiar with managing. Scribing created a safe pace to express and acknowledge his feelings. He eventually was able to write on his own, which was the goal. Establishing the safe path, the steps of the safe scaffolding was my role. It is the adult role. The guide sees the road and aids the child as they need with each step, releasing the assistance as the child is ready to make independent steps as the learner trusts the steps.

In the reference section of this book is a list of books I like and utilized in social-emotional teaching. This section is divided by developmental stages of picture books and then independent readers. I have used them one on one, as I read aloud books in large groups and reading groups always with lots of discussions.

Jacob kept a journal for drawings, and our feelings work together. I often planned writing prompts based on his social-emotional learning needs, current situations in his life at home and school, and the curriculum lessons.

Using authentic writing opportunities, I encouraged him to write letters to the principal with whom he had a special bond. The principal especially held Jacob and always went out of his way to check on him and his growth. The principal had been working with Jacob since he started school, and they had spent a lot of time together. Remember the magnet toy he had at his table? The principal had bought this gift for him after noticing Jacob enjoyed playing with this toy in the principal's office. Jacob earned this gift as a reward for not running from class and using the signal communication system for a few months. Jacob learned generosity, appreciation, and maintaining relationship skills through accountability behaviors and thank you card writing with the principal and other caring people in our community. After a few months, he began to notice people and situations he was grateful for on his own.

In the beginning, I would say things like, "That was so nice of Dr. Cross to notice you liked that puzzle and gave one to you for using your positive signals. Let's draw him one of your detailed pictures and write, 'Thank you to Dr. Cross.'" "That was so nice of Louise to make sure you had a sack lunch. Did you thank her?" "It made me smile to see Mr. Fox give you a high five this morning and compliment you playing fair in gym class." "How did you feel when Ms. Laurie gave you a Band-Aid after recess?"

Bringing to the surface, the community who cared for him was important. It challenged and changed some of the self-talk that kept him separate and alone and helped him accept his mother's absence and still feel safe. I wanted to build his community awareness and build his resilience. Teaching him appropriate relationship skills so he could maintain healthy relationships and give and receive love and support needed due to the crisis his family had been in for so long.

Jacob and I continued this phase of his work through third and fourth grade. During his fourth grade, he began to wean himself off my obvious attention in the mornings. My presence brought attention to him from his peers. This request was a success. He was nurturing his primary bond with his mother within himself and separating. I switched from our personal touch to leaving his snack on his desk before school started in the morning. By the end of the year, he no longer required a morning snack. During the two years he received this attention from me, I ensured that the days I was absent from school, another adult kept this commitment. The consistency was part of the healing. When I missed morning touch-based time because of unforeseen circumstances, we would discuss it during our problem-solving times, reminding him this was life. He had the resilience to cope and excellent emotional growth opportunities. His capacities were growing.

During the fall of his fifth grade Individual Education Plan Meeting, it was assessed that he was ready to join a literacy group with other fifth graders. I felt that our one-on-one sessions had served their purpose. He was stable and thriving in the classroom and at home. He still had a few slight hardships with literacy skills. The group he would join would serve these needs. Give him a chance to use his internalized positive primary bond transfer to strengthen his experience with secondary bonding with another teacher with excellent skills in teaching to his current growing needs. Joining this learning group would also be a chance for him to belong to a bunch of boys his age. Under her direction, this group broke down the concepts of writing and built them back up to support well-organized, rich paragraphs and essays and establishing independent and responsible behaviors required for the transition to middle school. I was still right next door and continued to check on him and available if needed and so proud of his growth.

By the end of fifth grade, he had completed all the goals of emotional tending. He had established relationship behaviors that served himself and his ability to maintain connections to others. He had reached grade-level academic expectations in all areas. Jacob was ready to leave special education services. In all my years in public education, Jacob was an example of a child with situational needs that our services were able to address and release. He and his father worked hard to accept the conditions of their lives. They came to appreciate the community. Jacob and his father knew Jacob's strengths and challenges. Isn't this what the human experience is about? Those of us with death in our lives as children just have the opportunity to get to work sooner.

The last time I saw Jacob was in the fall of his sixth grade year. The sixth graders had a free period every Wednesday. Jacob and a few friends came to visit us in elementary school. He came to my room with the sweetest, broad smile. He told all about how much he liked sixth grade. He asked how I was and the students in my class. He informed the kids he remembered drawing and writing in this class. He advised them to listen to Ms. Ryan. I could not have been prouder of the young man that stood before me: happy, confident, and able to have a reciprocal, caring relationship. So much healing from the wild, hurt child in the corner of the hall on the day we met.

"I believe the greatest gift I can conceive of having from
anyone is to be seen by them, heard by them, to be
understood and touched by them." Virginia Satir

Chapter
Five

Little Body, Big Emotions

The door opened and in stomped a small boy waving a piece of paper. He was screaming his angry words about his teacher. I gave him a slight nod to his privacy desk and set his timer for him. I made eye contact with my teacher assistant with a gentle reassurance that "we have this." The confidence that we can allow this child to experience his feelings and still have some sense of order in our learning environment. She returned her attention to the children that she was working with, and I returned to the paperwork I was working on, allowing this little boy of seven years old, five minutes to deescalate himself. He picked up the book he has chosen to be his calm-down book in his own space of the study carrel. Thumbing through this beloved book, through the pictures, he calmed himself down. This situation had been a daily routine throughout September as he and his teacher got to know each other. He had that "I got overstimulated in class" look. This little guy was a smart child with a series of mental illness diagnoses flying around him as the medical community tried to support him and his family. He often felt he knew better than his teacher. He did understand himself better. His teacher did not allow this type of disrespect or disruption in her class after 30 years of teaching.

In creating a plan of behavior modification required, I considered all the stakeholders in the elementary school, classroom, and child and his family. What was his behavior of tearing up his papers and yelling at his teacher communicating? How can other adults and I hear his needs, the teacher's and classroom needs and tend to them? He was an intelligent boy and wanted to learn in school. His mind moved fast with thoughts and rapid pictures increasing his over sensitivities within his nervous system, emotional body, and physical reactions.

The assessments, the prior special education team, passed on to me, showed me a lot of numbers to collaborate with my observations of him. I incorporated my intimate under-standing of the positive intention of human beings and many years of being with children with the standardized testing results and vast documented reports of other professionals.

This circumstance was my first year working at this school. They specifically hired me to integrate a program for children with intensive emotional needs and learning disabilities needs so that all the children could stay in their neighborhood elementary school. The children were to split their time between two classrooms: the general education classroom and the intensive/resource classroom depending on their ability to access the general learning environment and emotional needs programming. Therefore, they were members of both environments. The principal had gained a grant to address the unique needs in this school. My friend, who was retiring from a long career in special education, had recommended me for the job as I was finishing my master's program in 2003. We all were trying new support structures for this special population. These conditions allowed for creative problem solving for children with in-house administration support; however, I was creating a program by the seat of my pants, as fast I could with the team of a school psychologist, speech therapist, principal, and paraeducator. The general education teachers, while part of the children's program team, was understandably skeptical. The administration supported their concerns while requiring the program to be given some leeway, which included the kids and me. We had successes and challenges throughout that year.

This day, Joseph did not understand why he needed to follow through with the handwriting exercises of first grade. He had been seeing and doing these worksheets long enough. He had better ways to spend his time and had ideas to think about. Joseph was able to make this clear to us all angrily. "I have thinking to do," he yelled.

I had to consider the teacher's priorities, the first-grade curriculum and skill at hand, and the child's learning needs and style. Sometimes this means providing other learning material for the skill in question, or accommodations for the child's learning style to support reaching the lesson or assignment and following the classroom routine. Joseph had precise, legible handwriting. He can do worksheet practice, effortlessly. The skill we were working on for him was following classroom routine and tolerating disappointment and disagreement. Joseph and his teacher disagreed on how he should spend his time. The teacher expected the children to be doing the same activity at the same time in her direction without complaint. She has had this style in her classroom for a long time. I compassionately understood that the school environment had been changing significantly in the last years of her career. Also, I could appreciate Joseph's frustration. I hoped to support them both in coming to an understanding and some accommodation and compromises so Joseph could grow, and the teacher could feel respected and safe with a little change and lessen of control. We made suggestions for other writing practices he did alongside his peers.

I had evidence that his handwriting was growing nicely. I proposed to his classroom teacher. "How about some writing work that allowed his growing need to express himself with others? Let's give him some writing work that he needs practice with, such as spelling and noun, verb, adjective work?" The teacher agreed to me, creating a packet of work she could hand to him in times of need. He and I ended up co-creating his bundle of work, increasing his buy-in, and knowing his teacher and I were working with him. Joseph increased his willingness to worksheet work in class.

In Jacob's story, I used my therapeutic style of support. For many reasons, I addressed my participation with Joseph more at the skill level. Reasons being, Joseph was younger and already in treatment. The team I was working on had a school psychologist to take the lead for school therapeutics. I enjoyed collaborating and learning with her. I assessed myself, others, and the context to make my decisions with the team as to each of our roles. Joseph joined our boy's club to learn these skills.

The strategies the school psychologist introduced to our special resource classroom were the use of animal conflict styles to study metaphorically conflict options, a chance to understand our conflict style favorites, and maybe try on some new ones. To see which ones worked better for us or maybe different situations. And how people responded to different animal styles better than others. The team established a weekly class meeting with the students to explore the animal metaphors.

I will explain the techniques we used in our classroom. Upfront, this did not solve the angry outburst on the first day or even in the first month. We worked on learning and identifying these conflict styles all year. It takes time and practice to identify needs, feelings, and change behavior, so I again had our time out plan in place until de-escalation could happen at the moment with the child in the classroom.

The laminated animal cards with pictures and notes of their characteristics were beneficial for our visual learners and me. I was learning with the kids. Accessing the children's prior knowledge and interest in animals offered a rich context to learn about conflict and safely look at ourselves in a non-judgmental form. A shark is a shark. That is a way a shark is. Okay, when does it help to act like a shark? Is that the best way to solve every problem? Who is hurt with a shark attack? Do we want only to have shark ways, hurtful ways to solve problems? All the animals are part of the ecosystem and have a purpose. In our classroom, we needed to coexist and cooperate. How will we? Can we appreciate each style and learn together and practice taking risks and making choices?

As a teacher, it was fun to be learning with my students and assessing all the learning styles modeled with the animals, providing fun lessons with auditory, visual, and kinesthetic opportunities within the group and individual activities.

We did learn the shark and dog, first. The children we were working with, by definition, as being part of our emotional needs program, struggled with their tempers, shark attacks, wanting their way, and protecting themselves. And by definition, schools run better when we can work well in the pack, like the dog.

We also had dolphins, my personal favorite. Turtle/Ostrich, my under stress in hierarchical situations go to; a way to avoid conflict and stay safe. The fox who is compromising in a positive light and manipulative in sly dishonest light can create compromise. The owl who collaborates and thinks their idea is best. Here are the animal style descriptions.

Competing/Forcing (I Take Charge) -

Shark/Lion: aggressive, unpopular, makes necessary unpleasant decisions, leader, competitive, uses force and intimidation, strong survival instinct and attention to protection (boundaries), can harm relationships and blame. Favorite words are "My way!" demands the shark. Or "I know best," roars Lion.

Compromising (We meet halfway) -

Fox/Zebra: low impact compromises, tricky, manipulative, secretive, has many options, may compromise, tolerates, committed to finding a solution. Favorite words: "Let's listen to everyone's ideas and come to a solution we all are okay with," reasons the fox.

Accommodating (I give in) -

Dog/Chameleon/Teddy Bear: go along with the pack and the boss, playful, plays well with others, accommodating, tries to build harmony, we all have a job or role here, keeps the family together. Favorite words are, "Everything will be alright," soothes the Teddy Bear. "We can get along," puppy piles the dog.

Avoidance (I leave) -

Turtle: plodding, hides head in its shell or home, does not want to make the decision, avoids conflict, leaves and protects itself, placates, and tends to let others have their way. Favorite words are: "I don't care" "Don't ask me." "I don't want to be involved." "I'd rather not deal with it," hides the turtle.

Ostrich: puts head in the sand, avoids, never makes the hard decision, and denies there is a problem; wants to stay safe. Favorite words are, "I am fine with everything as it is." "There is not a problem," as the Ostrich digs deeper into its hole.

Collaborating (We both Win) -

Eagle: sees the big picture, does not sweat the small stuff, takes action when need be.

Owl: good for long term planning, team efforts, calm, thoughtful, collaborative, honesty is important, can be very heady and super reasonable. Favorite words are, "Here is the problem as I see it." "Let's try this solution." Cooperation dialogue: "My preference is... but what is yours?" encourages the owl.

Dolphin: playful, stays with the pods of dolphins, helpful, fun, and curious.

I write these descriptions based on my memory and current internet reminders. I do not know which organization the school psychologist I worked with used. I found the Young Peacemaker Project (cresst.or.uk) and Conflict Resolution Style Animals (https://creducation.net) helpful in filling in memory and providing specific descriptors.

Each conflict style has positive and negative qualities and can be understood and used for appropriate situations. Once we know all the conditions and purposes of the methods and how we perceive them within ourselves, we can choose to utilize those that suit our best interests and the situation. Choices were the goal we had in teaching these skills and creating pause and options within the children.

The children learned the level of safety and discerned if there was a risk in the situation or whether it was in the students' best interest to be vulnerable as part of their learning. Bringing the discussion and learning out of the heat of the moments into a circle of safety and practicing the styles in role-plays increased the cognitive choices the children had during their daily upsets and stressors.

The children had journals for their self-reflections and homework done in the resource classroom for Friday meeting time. I found a list in one of my journals from 2/2/2004.

The title of the Journal page was:

Journal Ideas:

Positive Energy Moments

Positive Self Talk

How I used animal strategies to solve problems positively.

How I made problems bigger with my animal strategy choices.

*Homework: Write about other animals and read four in circle Friday. Justin and Raul will read three when Dr. V. comes to class.

During our team meeting, we would discuss and collaborate ideas for the week as well as long-term progress. I like how, even in our group, we modify the expectations for the students' reading and writing level abilities.

Haikus

We had quiet time to write poetry. Using the five-seven-five syllable structures of haiku, we described our favorite animals. In my journal at that time, I wrote:

Good morning sweet child
Swirling, jumping adventure
Love with another

Sunrises to greet
The water shines Blue, Bright and Gold
Warm and Cool to Touch

Teenagers at play
Parents watching, play and joy
Belly to Belly

Can you guess which animal was inspiring my haikus?

Other examples of animal poems:

These are my waters,
I live here,
Who are you? I am hungry!
Chomp, Chomp, Chomp, Sigh.

Not now, Not ever, ever.
I go inside and hide long,
My hard shell stays safe.

I dig deep in sand
Where it is safe, cool always.
I look funny but blind.

Stay calm.
Calmly, speak the words,
Look around check out details,
I have the ideas.

Roam in the shadows,
Seeing all at night.
Possibilities Abound,
I will find a way.

Soft, Cuddly Soft
Squeeze me, feel better, be okay.
Your way is my way.
Squeeze me tight and feel better.

Play with me, throw a ball.
Give me a job, throw a ball.
What is my job, best friend?
Jobs direct my energy!
Hip Hip Hooray, Chip!

Temperature Reading

On Fridays, we had a group meeting and learning time with the students in our program to bond, create safety, problem solve, and learn these skills of emotional equilibrium and communication. We had three to four adults to seven to ten students in our weekly meetings.

Virginia Satir introduced a modality to bring a group to the present moment and build relationships through allowing our humanness to be honored and expressed. Our team accommodated several modalities to use during our circle. We brought the intent of the temperature reading into our classroom meetings with adjustments for our culture and time limits. Virginia introduced the temperature reading, starting with appreciations, which positively opens the sharing safety net. With the children, which happened to be a boys group, we began with bragging.* What they appreciated about themselves. We adults were part of the group and circle, so we participated with the children. The warmth and wiggles we all felt seeing each other brag nourished our community and increased everyone's awareness of the resources we contributed and could lean into during hard times of learning challenges, family conflicts, peer conflicts, and negative self-talk.

Satir followed her temperature reading with worries and concerns. These are feelings and thoughts of situations that weigh heavy on our minds and hearts, yet there are no actions. For our version of worries and concerns in the classroom we reframed to fears. Given the harshness of the environment, many of the boys lived in, it was not safe to express fears, so we as adults would speak and model small fears that were relatable to school. Sometimes, we would reframe and identify their stories revealing their possible fears by saying, "I would feel afraid in that situation." As the year went on, trust and safety increased, and the boys would share more.

Next, the temperature reading has problems with solutions. Virginia felt that the person with the problem usually had the solution. With the opportunity to discuss problems in a circle and offer a solution to the group, the children modeled positive conflict resolution. They had time to practice working as a kind group towards a healthy learning environment. At this time, the adults would introduce the lesson we had planned during our team meeting earlier in the week. These lessons included describing the animals' styles, identifying the animals in our group and situations at school and home. Through academic and experiential learning lessons we taught social skills.

We finished our circle with gratitude and one goal for the next week. Virginia finished her temperature reading with hopes and wishes to help individuals identify and voice their desires and have the community witness and support the individual in their growth toward their dreams and wishes. A spiritual piece of speaking to the universe and making preferences more likely to happen. I have noticed once I express my hopes, desires, goals, and gratitude, I know when to say "yes" and when to say "no" more clearly, matching my behaviors, aligning my plans and hopes and dreams. I noticed the opportunities in my life more and stayed on my path. Oprah says, "I feel that luck is a preparation meeting opportunity."

In our program, we had worksheet contracts with the students with their goals, plans to reach their goal and feedback space for the steps witnessed towards their goals. The boys earned points towards Friday Rewards when staying on track and "caught being good." The adults practiced looking for what the children were doing right and brought attention to those moments, and soon the boys learned to notice for themselves and each other. We divided the days into a.m. and p.m., so if one had a bad morning the whole day or week, it was not ruined and for not. The students had a chance to turn their behavior and day around, with support to succeed in their goals. Even a few students had the time tables delineated by subject times or 45 minuntes. Depending on the pendulum, the student fell in outburst or not doing school work and behaviors of positive learning. The charts represent their maturity and need for restarts and positive feedback.

All these strategies fit into the discussion of helping children with grief because often grief is expressed through behaviors not conducive to the learning environment and challenging communication. All of the children in this special program, created for them, had one or several of the following situations in their environments: mental illness in self or parent, addictions in the family system, death of a family member, murder of a family member, incarceration of a family member, dangerous immigration stories and families left behind. Also, discrimination, poverty, poor nutrition, and maternal care during pregnancy, and organic learning disabilities and environmental induced learning challenges. Loss and grief and handling those through anger, violence, and depression were part of daily life.

Peace Place

Our school utilized the Peace Place Mediation. The skills for Peace Place had to be taught explicitly. Peace Place can be a specific place like a table or bench or designated location with a sign and agreement to follow the Peace Place Process to give every voice a chance to be heard during problem-solving. Talking was an alternative to fighting. Our students were expected to use this process on the playground and were failing. We decided to include teaching and practicing the process until our boys were the leaders in Peace Place on the playground. We practiced with made up funny problems, real classroom situations, family disagreements with siblings, and playground scenarios. Several times a week, authentic in-the-moment situations popped up, and we practiced Peace Place. First, the children decide to solve their conflict at Peace Place. Each student tells what happened from their point of view. After the children state the problem from all points of view, the Peer Mediator asked each to give their ideas for a solution. Finally, the meditator repeats the ideas until a solution is agreed upon. In our practices in the classroom and on the playground, we had adult facilitators to support the process as part of the explicit teaching methods. I have a note from 2/2004, with the suggestion to help the family of Justin design a Peace Place Practice in their home.

To end this story on a high note, one of the adult team members was a British citizen with dual citizenship. She brought with her personal and cultural resources of hard work ethic, manners, and tea time. As we progressed, she increased her dedication to our boy club. She shared more and more of herself. Our boys were very food motivated. She introduced Friday Tea Time for us to relax and connect and nourish together. The boys earned this time with their feedback goal charts. While giving her generosity of organizing and offering the tea time with her teapot, she also demanded we follow the protocols she raised. This sharing of other family styles and childhood memories model for the club different family structures and expect-ations. She taught us how the pourer of the tea was called Mother and the etiquette of afternoon tea. Being the "no nonsense lady" she was, she would not allow poor behavior. Think of Mary Poppins. It gave a window into what the boys were capable of in respect and dignity. Boy, they loved Ms. Vicky and tea time. They worked hard to earn Friday Tea. We all went home on Friday on a high note of high tea.

"Problems are not the problem; coping is the problem."
Virginia Satir

*I credit the renaming of Temperature Reading's Appreciations to Bragging for children to a conversation with a colleague, Tim Brod MA., who used this technique in the Glenn County Mental Health Program.

Chapter

Six

Pissed Off

On a trip to Montana in the mid-90s, my husband and I stayed with a friend who had a litter of kittens born to a feral mother under her house. While we played scrabble one night with friends, we decided that we would take one of the kittens home. Our family had recently lost our old cat, and our daughters had lost another cat during the influx of new people into our neighborhood. One white kitten returned with us to Colorado and was named Marie. Since we had lost a cat, our daughter was afraid to allow this cat outside, which was an upfront challenge with a feral cat, taming and training her into a house cat. I had only had cats that were allowed in and out. With all the emotional needs of loss with our daughter from the last pets and her young age, her ability to build a relationship with this animal was affected. Our daughter did not read the cues of the cat well. We often heard screams and tears after the cat had enough and escaped the child's arms. Yes, yes, yes, now I look back at what a crazy situation this was. I hope I would do it differently now, but my lack of ability to allow my girls their feelings of loss and thinking I had to smooth things over and fix loss, I jumped into a replacement pet that caused a great deal of trouble. I was not up to tending to the introduction of a traumatized animal into our home. All my other cats up to this point had been inside and outside cats and joined the surroundings readily. I had to learn more, so I added to my chaos. These hardships provided learning for me and gave me insights later.

Marie began peeing on the carpet in our daughter's bedroom. She would sit on the window sill and look out the window. I think to try to be as close to outside as possible. She was peeing on the carpet and ruining the floor and baseboards. We tried everything we could think of, to no avail, to clean the area and change the cat's behaviors, except what she wanted, which was to go outside.

I was beginning to get quite frustrated and had never had this experience with a cat before. It was more than I signed up for. A friend of mine visited, who has a good sense of people and animals. We were complaining about the cat. He asked to see where the cat was peeing. When our friend looked out the window and noticed another cat, The neighbor cat was walking back and forth on the fence we shared with our neighbors. Our cat often sat in this window next to the screen in the spot near where she peed. Well, have you ever heard of the term "pissed off"? Our friend said he thought our cat was being teased by the cat on the fence and feeling territorial and not allowed outside and "pissed off."

That cat was still challenging to train. After that observant- ion and insight into the motive of the cat's behavior, we placed a litter box under the window. The new placement of the litter box helped a lot. It helped to figure out which rooms in the house the cat was less agitated; rooms she could not see the outside cat. We had more understanding and compassion for the cat that helped with the problem- solving in her training. We were addressing the deeper issue.

Today this story reminds me of a foster child and his family I once worked for. I met this family at school, and they were in the process of adopting this little boy. He was in preschool and age four, almost five. The child came to live with his foster family when his own family wasn't able to continue to care for him. During his formative years, he was severely neglected and abused. The birth parent would tell him he had to stay in his bedroom for long stretches at a time. He could not leave his room. They trained him to pee in the corner of his room by locking his door. When he first came to his new home, he was still peeing in the corner of his bedroom, which was a surprise to new parents because he was toilet trained during the day time and in preschool. They were slowly able to reassure him and permitted him to go to the bathroom whenever he needed to without getting in trouble. His need to urinate in his bedroom ended.

Another habit began. The child started to wander around the house at night and went downstairs to eat sugary treats while the rest of the family slept. This behavior escalated to waking the other children in the home in the middle of the night to play. Often after introducing new children into a family when one situation is addressed, another one rises, a game of whack-a-mole, as the child gains safety and is in the process of healing traumas. The parents began waking in the early hours of darkness to the children running around the house. They would put the children back to bed and tell them it was not morning yet and go back to sleep. They made sure the little boy got enough food during the day. He continued to wake each night until the whole family was sleep deprived and frustrated. The parents were at a loss of what to do.

One morning, the foster mother brought the child to school. She was so upset. "I just do not know what we are going to do." she confided in me.

The parents had shared their concerns and struggle with this nighttime behavior during parent conferences. The mother gave me the short version of how their morning started without hiding how upset she was.

The mother had made it clear to the little boy at home he needed to remain in his room and not wake others up until the father was up for work at 6:00 a.m. They had plenty of food for him during the day. Night hunger was not a reason for him to leave his room. The family was expecting another child, and there were other stress factors in the home. This morning the situation hit an emotional outburst. The boy had peed in his room on the floor, and when the mother went in to get him ready for school, she stepped in the wet spot on the carpet and screamed with shock.

When the mother had asked him at home, "Why did you pee in your bedroom?" he kept saying, "I don't know. I don't know." Until he yelled, "You are so mean. You won't let me leave my room at night. I am not supposed to leave my room."

I realized he was angry and reminded me of the feral cat we had in our home so many years before. I remembered the power of naming "Pissed off."

I watched the child's face as the mother told me how their day had started. She was hurt. He began to show signs of remorse and shame, seeing how upset his mother was.

I turned my attention to him and spoke my observations. The child could see her tears of frustration. I was able to calmly have the mom sit down and watch me work with the child. Labeling what I could name and seeing him, and validating, "Little one, you matter." "Your behavior makes a difference." and "You are powerful."

I gently began to process what I saw in him and the situation:

"You know how to fix where you pee?"

He nods his head, "Yes."

"You know where the right place is to pee?"

"Yes," he said.

"You see, your behavior affects Mommy. She is having feelings." He continued to nod his head.

"Do you still want to do that?"

"No," he shook his head.

"Is it harder to know what to do when you are angry and hurt?"

"Did you feel pissed off this morning and pee on the carpet?"

"Yes," with a wide-eyed nod to the recognition of his anger.

His shame was powerful. I invited him into my lap and arms. I held him like a two-year-old. This behavior lived in his young experience. He learned helplessness, control, and power around his toilet training. He was regressing with the new stress in the family and boundaries to his freedoms. The mother began to breathe deeper.

We could hear his communication now. Through her foster son's behavior, he was telling us he was angry and scared. He felt he didn't matter. He needed to be seen and known that he mattered to others and had choices. He affected those around him, especially his mother. Slowly, he was able to acknowledge how sorry he was and sad that mommy was mad. He had the power to fix where he peed. He was able to ask if he and mommy were okay. He heard me ask Mommy if she still liked and loved him to reassure his unspoken question if he still belonged.

Mommy was able to thank him for his apology and assure him, and they were okay. She still had a few more things to make sure he understood, so I held the bridge and safety for them to work it out further.

Interesting how animals supply insight into our children and source human behaviors. The metaphors and idioms we have in our languages: pissed off, pecking order, and coyote crazy. This child was slowly recovering from the lack of control he experienced during his early years, and how to have a sense of control and choice. The time now was to teach him; he mattered. He was safe. And help him respond to situations when he felt out of control and angry with better options.

"Before we give people help, we need to know what kind they need." Virginia Satir

Chapter

Seven

Power of Friendship, Ritual, Dreams, and Literature

A dear woman and friend of mine passed this weekend. We were colleagues as well as women on a similar path. When she became ill this past summer, I immediately felt the devastating impact on her family and realized the depth of a quiet treasure she was. The aspect of grief that teaches us to be grateful and honor our relationships and the human strengths we have in our lives before the inevitable loss was significant in the moment for both of us. She spoke of the hopes she previously had for her future that would not come. The most precious was being a grandmother. The sadness as she accepted that if her children were graced with children of their own, she would not be there and miss these moments. As an adult daughter without her mother, I identified with her children intensely and felt what the deep loss this will be.

This friend had supported me through times when my female friends filled the void of not having the continued mothering I craved and gave me love and guidance. At this moment, with her passing, her gifts are ever evident. I trusted her to tend and be available to my pregnant daughter when I was called out of the country during her pregnancy. This friend responded to my request for a women's circle for my daughter to know my friends were there to be called on while I was gone. This is one of the many ways this gracious woman let me and many know she thought of them and considered how she could love them better. Twelve women were invited to the women's circle by my friend. Sage and incense were burned to clear the space. She planned sacred space making with rose water for washing our hands and faces as we came into the circle. We each brought items to remind the young mother of her own resources, including our friendships, flowers, beads for a friendship necklace, rose lotion and bath supplies, nursing gowns, and baby outfits. We went around the circle, sharing poems and wisdom pieces that each of us as mothers enjoys supporting our motherhood. We sang a few songs. Each woman fully stated she was willing and hoping to support my daughter now and in the future journey of motherhood. We closed the circle by saying prayers to all mothers and children and joined in a potluck of food and tea.

Many layers of healing rained on me as I witnessed and participated in the conscious dying process my friend orchestrated and asked for. When the end of treatment was given, she went home, and space was created in the living room for her care and final closing space. The sanctuary created was palpable. Visitors were welcomed and invited. The community responded with meal deliveries and loving visits. The artwork she gained beauty and strength from hung from the mantel. The music she cherished in the background. The fire in the fireplace framed the hearth and heart. The prayer circle brought a hand-knitted afghan to keep her warm and beautiful. Life slowed to her speed. She had always reminded me of the turtle for her depth like the Mother Earth and thoughtful response time to life. She picked the medicine card Turtle with her pastor. Comfortable chairs surrounded the bedside for her final visits and laid the circle of energy for when we were there for the vigil following her death.

She requested three days of vigil to be sat during the time of her spirit movement and the long goodbye for her loving husband and three children. This was a practice she had studied and utilized around her father's death several years before giving her family an image to follow in her time. We all spoke of how nurturing this experience was for each of us. New images and experiences of death were given. Her grace in accepting her illness and for seeing death coming and doing her own work to completion laid a fertile path for us to follow and rest in as we said goodbye and felt the sadness and appreciation of all she was to us.

While living this ritual with her, I began to have a deep awareness of her virtues and love. I was in the rewrite stage of this book and had days and more of stuckness. I was not able to write during the two weeks of her hospice care. I felt the depth of energy, creativity, life force, and physical need to hold space for her dear soul and family. I breathed with them across the town. I practiced yoga with them in my heart. I honored her gifts to me. I stood in truth to be kind and giving during this time. And I worried about the timeline I had set for this book.

The sleep following her leaving her body, I had a powerful dream. I woke up at the time she had stopped breathing the 24 hours before. I felt anxious and concerned. I consider what I need to do. Thinking maybe I would go right then to her, I began meditating and sending energy to the vigil holders. As I fell back to deep rest, I dreamed. When I woke a second time, I struggled to rise and tend to the day and picked up the room that a guest coming to pay her respects would stay. The books I listed in the resources of this book lay on the floor in front of the bookshelf in the grandchildren's room, which also was used as a guest room and my yoga spot. I picked up the books to reshelve: next right thing. As I held the book, *Heckedy Peg's* energy and weakness shook me. I just remembered my mother had spoken to me in a dream hours before, and on her list of wisdom, she had written *Heckedy Peg*. I began remembering this dream—the feelings and details and synchronicities.

Heckedy Peg has been a favorite book of mine to read with children since my daughters. I believe in the power of folk and fairy tales. While watching my second granddaughter daily for her nap time, we fell into the pattern of reading this book. She requested it each day and began to chant and repeat the speech of the mother, children, and witch in the book with me, asking to role play parts, asking to do the knock on the door to the point it was clearly her favorite story, and it spoke to her on many levels, as fairy tales do. They address our deepest fears and are multi-leveled in consciousness. Today I marveled at how the story was speaking in my dream. As I practiced my yoga and spoke of my dream in a sacred circle, the impact and meaning to be connected to the power of motherly love, of a mother seeing and knowing her child and protecting them as two of the lessons and themes in the *Heckedy Peg* book. Weaving my friend's death with my mother's visit in my dream with this spiritual literature nourished me and gave insight into the project of helping children with grief and healing as a helper.

In the dream, my mother was the age she was when she died. I was my current age. We had a conversation woman to woman about our learning and experiences. I remembered feeling the kinship of adult female relationships happening between us and how special that was for me to feel. Then she handed me a note with three lessons she was learning. While I was not able to remember the first two while recalling the dream, I remember the third.

"Like *Heckedy Peg*."

I said to my mother, astonished, "You know *Heckedy Peg* is Avery's favorite book."

She shook her head, "No, I do not know because I have not been here," with sadness.

Truth and reality, spirituality, and magic, all collided bringing acceptance and healing for me. The love reality of which we are all one and connected to the one spirit and heart of breath. Our helpers and friends are all around, loving us as we need. My friend had the gift of seeing others. She felt and shared my experience as a daughter longing for her mother and filling a space for me.

Of course, she knows, and I know, and we are all connected in spirit. There will be sadness in the loss of these bodies and touch. We miss the ease of being supported by each other during the acceptance of the loss. We will continue the inspiration of connection and one breath. Thank you, dear friend.

Heckedy Peg listed on the reference page.

Chapter

Eight

Sacred Pictures

Avery's Process

My granddaughter, at five years old, liked to take photos with our cell phones and look through our photo galleries discussing memories with us. It was natural to use her hobby as a window into sacred actions for her. The week their roommate died of a tragic, unexpected car accident, her dad sent me a collection of pictures of this beautiful friend who had shared so many family celebrations over the last three years, over half of my granddaughter's life.

My son-in-law was his roommate's emergency contact, and when the phone call came in from the police, Avery was resting on his lap watching a movie with her dad. She witnessed the tragic phone call and soaked in the energetic pain around her, adding to her fear and sadness. We are a close family and share in child care duties and needs. Her father called me right away to meet them at the hospital to pick up Avery so the adults could tend to the emergency. When my husband and I arrived, it was clear to our son-in-law, the accident was terrible, and his dear friend may not make it. He handed our granddaughter to Popi, and Jarrod fell into my arms. While it was overwhelming for us all, I had concerns for my granddaughter witnessing this all. Later, I was proud that her father showed his emotions and showed receiving support.

We took Avery to our farm and allowed any expressions she needed. As children often do, she began processing through play with us nearby to reflect her play back to her. We received the news that our friend did not make it through the accident. We met our adult daughter and another granddaughter for dinner. At this point, the children knew of the accident, and Patrick was in the hospital. Our daughter wanted to wait to tell the children after they were home about his passing.

We stayed close as a family over the weekend, sharing meals. The children were aware that when their parents spoke of the roommate or the children spoke of the roommate, adults cried. The children were deciding it was wrong to talk about the friend. It was incredible from my witnessing eyes to see how children navigate family structures and internalize the unspoken rules through their developmental ages. Avery asked me to go to the bathroom with her. It turned out she needed to speak in private, and this is where I found out what was going on. With young children, it is often in the bathroom ritual where we, as caregivers, learn the underneath of a child's process, just as it is in the car for middle school children.

She looks at me seriously, "Do you know Patrick died?"

"I know, sweetheart."

"Who told you?" She demanded.

"Mommy," I answered.

"Mommy told me too," She told me.

"Addy says not to talk about Patrick because it makes Daddy and Jennie cry," she confided in me.

"Oh, Honey, we all are going to cry because it is very sad. We can talk about it."

"No! We can't," she threatened.

"Okay, Honey. Do you want a hug?" I asked.

"Un-huh," she nods her head, "Yes."

When we went back to the table, I confidently brought up Patrick's name to my son-in-law and his girlfriend. The adults began sharing memories while the children watched with big eyes and colored the restaurant menus. I allowed some tears to roll down my face, and then the other adults began showing their feelings. We even had a few laughs through the tears of funny things Patrick did with the kids like having a bike race with daddy on the kids' bikes. My husband and I were conscious of the process this little household was going through. Our own experiences being slightly removed, our sadness was not cutting as deep as the grief of those who were Patrick's family for the last three years. We were able to navigate the feelings with some detachment and care.

Our family is a multi-generational blended family. My husband, Popi, as the grandkids call him, is my second husband and our daughters' stepdad. We have navigated families separating and blending up close. When our daughter married young, we were very involved in supporting her family unit and our son-in-law. When it was time for them to separate from each other as man and wife, we all stayed close because that was right for us. I refer to my grandchildren's father as my son-in-law because, in my heart, he still is one of mine.

However, my daughter requires another relationship and boundary, so when she called a few days later to say the kids were rough, I said, "Come for a visit to the farm."

When they showed up, the kids were having explosive feelings and not listening to Mom. Popi always has something to do outside and asked the kids if they wanted to help a bit so I could sit with Momma. She filled me in on how it has been, and we got connected. My daughter and I are very close, and she knows my priorities and skills. When the kids came back in the house, they were expressing anger at each other and at Mom. As a social worker and teacher, I could see the anger as the first layer covering grief and the family structural dynamic. I decided to intervene with love and support. Their mom was pleased to have me do some "Meme Magic."

"Avery, I have something to show you in your room."
She growled at me.

I walked into the bedroom and pulled out some new colored pencils she had not seen yet. She stomped her feet as she followed me and jumped on the bed. We began coloring. I asked how she has been.

"Addy and I are mad that Patrick died. Why didn't that garbage truck STOP! Daddy is mad at the truck driver too," she told me.

"I know, Honey." I breathed with her, allowing what needed to come forward to come. She told me more.

After a while, I said, "Daddy sent me some pictures of Patrick. Would you like to see them?"

She nodded her head, "Yes."

I pulled out my phone, and she took it into her hands and scrolled through as she has done on so many occasions when missing Mommy and Sissy.

Avery began to describe the pictures. She said, "Daddy and Patrick on Christmas morning; Patrick in the bouncing house on my birthday; Patrick and Todd on Addy and my bicycles." She laughed at how funny it was to see the bike too small for Patrick.

I asked, "Would you like to draw a picture for Patrick?"

Nodding again, She started drawing, then she asked for my help. She wanted the drawings to depict the photographs. She began to direct me on how to draw and on what to portray. She was dictating to me as so many children in preschool, kindergarten, and special needs classrooms have done with me before. I felt her desire. I understood her needs to document their shared history. Her memories tender with her anger at the loss presented and relived the life, love, and fun they shared. I continued to be her scribe, her agent of expression holding her tender space to feel and love moving under the anger and sadness to know her experience with Patrick had been real. She could feel her feelings and be okay that her feelings did not harm me. I was falling in love with her sharing and expression.

Again, I am someone connected to her, yet I have a level of detachment from the intensity of feeling in this situation. I can see and hold and pursue her genius as an expression of healing. She intuitively knew how to express and heal and follow the desire to do so. Children intuitively know how to heal. I believe this about children—their wisdom connected to the Higher Power of sacredness. My experience shows me to trust, breathe, and follow as I guide and set safe structures for the children.

She told me the words that go with each picture. We concluded with five recreation pictures of Patrick with the family, a little book of memories for Avery. She was very proud of our pictures and showed the rest of the family. Sacred Pictures, healing, and allowing the family to grieve and smile of the love shared with these precious members' loss.

Following are the black and white images Avery and I made to honor and remember Patrick.

Images for Patrick

Avery drew Patrick a picture of a flower.

This is Chip. He is pushing Patrick
on Avery's fast bike.

Patrick and Dad, Dad is holding Decker when Dad proposed to Jen.

Avery,
Me, Dad, and Jen, Addy and Patrick are at the fair.

It is Halloween with Avery, Patrick
our roommate, Dad, & Jen.

Daddy and Patrick on Christmas morning.

Chapter
Nine

Farm Healing

Chickens, Drums, and Nature

Next how to help big Sissy?! I worked with the little sister through drawing to support her grief. Big Sissy needed another approach to acknowledging her grief. She was on the verge of eight. Addy has an aliveness that asks questions about the natural world and how things work. She is deeply connected to her Native American and Irish roots on a cellular level without the direct teachings in our family.

The house was filled with little sis and momma, so I said, "Addy, your turn, let's go out to the chicken coop."

Here is some back story. We moved to a farm five years ago because of the following spirit and grace. I had no idea that my retirement would be on a farm. However, the power that guides said, "Look, grandchildren are being born. Your husband is an amazing beekeeper. The house on the hill sold at the same time the county approved your bid on five acres of open space. Small farm, beekeeper's wife it is."

I started my farm soul investment with chickens. The baby chicks were so fun in the grass with two-year-old Addy in the spring. Building a coop, learning the chicken's ways and needs, and many social structures with the flock were entertainment for me. I would sit in the run and just watch and enjoy the chicken's interactions. I was still teaching and would share with my students the chickens' escapades, using photos from the farm as writing prompts, sharing chicken metaphors in staff meetings, examining chicken idioms with my students learning English. The farm was tapping into my soul, my childhood memories, and my ancestors.

I incubated eggs the next spring, and through grace, the grandchildren were here the day the chicks began to hatch. We squealed in delight and danced around the kitchen. Only one chick matured enough to survive, so we kept her in the house with us to keep a close eye on her and give her social interactions. She was our first Rosie. Addy loved the name, Rosie.

That summer, a long-time dream of my father and I came true. Spotting a trip to Ireland that included a condo stay in the small town of Adare for ten days within our budget, we planned our trip to see the land of our ancestors.

Our lodging was a short drive from the small town my dad's grandfather was born, Bird Hill. My great grandfather was a faulkner of the manor house. As we sat on the rock marking the village of Bird Hill, I felt with amazement the full circle that had landed my father and me here. I felt the power of ancestry, whether I consciously know or not. My chicken joy, my chicken care was beginning to take on more meaning and understanding. It is in my blood to care for birds. I was following a deep family lineage without even knowing it.

Then we went to a historical village with recreated homes of times passed for the Irish. Standing in a peat miner's hut, my dad recalled his grandfather's night dreams of being called out by his father to get the peat. Sacred memories surrounded us. We walked into a farmer's home, which held a chicken box in the kitchen.

I innocently said, "Oh curious, they kept their chickens in the kitchen."

My husband laughed and said, "Like us."

I didn't even realize that I was doing the same thing back home. Rosie was in our kitchen. The unconscious is a powerful guide.

Fast forward to when I faced another powerful loss. My support network suggested I create a grieving tent for myself outside, so I could honor my grief and stay present to my feelings. It was natural for me to turn to the chicken coop. There was an entry to the building that held my chickens. I hung a large scarf to separate some space. I brought things that comforted me and supported my grief: my drum, sage, candles, pillows, blankets, a rocking chair, a journal, tissues, and water. I committed to my therapist to daily time in my grieving space. I found with regular attention to my feelings that I experienced freedom through the other parts of my day. Where I had been experiencing my grief sneaking up on me and feeling overwhelmed; this changed as I attended to my feelings. When they arose, I felt some sense of manageability with my feelings and currentness with my daily life routines.

This was where I brought my granddaughter, experiencing her first big loss through death. To share with her the womanly art of tending to one's self and feelings. I shared why I place these objects in the room, why I come to the chicken coop, what I do in the chicken coop. I had her light one of our beeswax candles we made together from the wax Popi gathered. I showed her how to light the sage and spread its smoke through space. I began to drum and sing. I spoke my truth around my feelings of loss. She began to drop her shoulders, express tender pinkness in her checks, shy glances from her eyelids. We were together in this space, held and okay while being a little weird and new. Addy let me know she was ready to close her grief time. I saluted with the drum.

She said, "Meme, let's go hold Rocky." Rocky was this season's teenage chicken. I smiled.

As she held Rocky, she said she wished she could hold her chicken every morning to start her day like me.

I said, "Yes, that would be nice. You have Rhett, the family dog."

"Could you pet and lay with Rhett each morning to remember?"

"Yes, Meme, I could. I will try."

She was ready to meet this present moment, to be with Mommy and Sissy again. This was the day the universe let me know it was time to write a book about sacred actions.

"We need four hugs a day for survival. We need eight hugs a day for maintenance. We need twelve hugs a day for growth." Virginia Satir

Chapter Ten

Grieving Tent

Sacred Tantrums

Me in my grieving tent.

What a wild heart unleashed in my therapist's office that morning. The feelings of the soul hurt that needed to be expressed more and heard more. Sounds from deep inside rose as I bowed to the ground. As I hit the pillows with my tennis racket given to me by my dear sacred healing sister.

"How dare my love be abused and used!"

After years of accountability work, I bottled up the raw outrage of betrayal and loss. The deep pain that still lived in my cells and had not been voiced rose at this moment of saying goodbye to the treasure that bound us. She had so much energy, this hurt, and grief. So much power that it needed to be used to birth my purpose; to take my seat of being a woman of a certain age. Without tapping into the deepest loss of love, my soul had experienced shrinking each day, getting smaller by not acknowledging the truth beneath and inside me. I hid this rage to protect myself and my daughters, out of my fear of the power of this raw, truthful energy.

Now I needed to rise to the position of Grandmother. This time with wisdom, with trials and years behind me and sitting on the throne left empty by my maternal lineage.

Recognizing the nurturance of the power energy to feed my body and soul as I become the spiritual being of my own universe.

Reliable as a truth speaker

Reliable as a presence of love and authenticity

The young woman and small child spoke to me now in the screams and tears that there are problems, but I am not a problem. My feelings are not the problem.

ALLOW, Allow, allow, and accept my feelings.

Under the guidance of my sacred helper, my therapist, my chicken coop, became my grieving tent. A space of safety and sacredness for me to cleanse my shoulders of should and shouldn't and bring forth the deepest of wounds and feelings on purpose. On purpose to learn my truths, to hear the wisdom that was inside that my good girl fears repressed and my social conditioning had denied. I needed this time to tap into what this grief had to teach me and move through the intensity and mess with allowances. To grow the fearlessness of my feelings and other feelings. To connect to a power stronger than my ego. To be able to tend to myself and have boundaries with the day to day demands and change the parts of my path and future that I could and needed to change. The opportunity was overwhelming. The overwhelm was saying to listen. "When are you going to listen and take care of yourself?"

The grieving tent is taking care of one's self. A step and boundary that I matter, my feelings matter, my love and loss matters, my health matters, and to serve the universe better, I need this tending. To live better, I needed this tending. To live longer, I needed this learning. I need to teach this lesson, so learn this lesson.

My therapist asked me questions, knowing I lived in an open space with a pasture. "Could you pitch a tent on a corner of the property? Could you make a place where you could be alone out of earshot and not be watched? Can you not drive and take care of the children for two weeks?"

"Why?"

"I want you to make space to allow the grief to be felt. It should be outside away from your family. Your own space for this purpose."

"Okay, I know where that is. It is in my chicken coop, and that is easy." I can do that on my own.

The coop has two rooms and a roost. The front room which I made comfortable with a rug, rocking chair, candles, sage, daily inspirational books, pillows, and the gifted tennis racket I had learned to use and trust in my therapist's office.

What a shift to give permission to the feelings at a dedicated time daily instead of constant avoidance and surprise and take over of the feelings; instead of the low grade of depression and anger. The surprising experience of feelings that once I routinely felt them, the intensity lessened. The ability to have choice around my feelings increased. My availability to it and the life around it increased. The dread was lifted. I was empowered.

I am setting the boundary that I am tending to my relationship with myself and my love relationship to a dear one who has died. I will not drive for two weeks. I will only do what is absolutely necessary to maintain my life and family. In conversation with my family, I spoke about what this time is. This is what you can expect. I asked if they could support me. The relief of my family that I was communicating honesty, and taking care of myself was affirming. This was the right action for this time.

Little did we know that I was preparing myself and lifestyle for this book and the pandemic quarantine, building itself for this moment.

Chapter

Eleven

The Feelings Circle

When the granddaughters were four and seven, it was arranged to have Popi and I watch them and enjoy the evening together so their parents could enjoy the night in adult manners. The girls arrived with all kinds of plans and expectations for the evening. Popi and I could get on board with some of the hopes for the evening, some not and some we will see. Sleepovers and holidays are frothed with opportunities for unmet expectations. With excitement and watchful apprehension, we stepped into the sweet chaos.

As the night darkened, and sleepiness broached our home, disappointment and anger reared their ugly heads. The kids were getting tired. At a point, I thought to myself, "Okay, okay, okay. Let's deal with these emotions. What is wrong?"

I had been learning in my own emotional healing that emotions are energies that last 90 seconds when allowed to be felt in a supportive environment. Feelings when allowed to be acknowledged and felt, move, and change more rapidly. The four-year-old had run to the bedroom and slammed the door.

I waited a few moments and then went to the door, knocked, and said, "I was coming in."

She was throwing her toys. I sat down on the floor and asked her, "What was wrong, and what did she need?"

She yelled some more. It appeared to me that this tantrum was not only about this moment. A big, deeper conflict was being expressed. She was hurt and not able to talk about it.

I remembered a strategy that I had read about before and used in my own therapy. While I am not a therapist, I am someone who loves this child and has more maturity and insight. It is New Year's Eve, so my choices were what they were.

I decided to follow my gut and own experience and gave her a pillow and a tennis racket and said, "Here, hit the pillow and tell the pillow all you are mad about." She looked at me with a "Really?" look.

I said, "Really, just get it out."

She tentatively hit the pillow then got stronger and stronger.

I asked, "What words go with this feeling?" Slowly, angry words came out.

I continued to say, "Good, let it out of your body."

While some of the feelings and words were heartbreaking for me to hear, I continued to remain as unemotional and detached as possible and kept a safe container for her release. She began to lose steam, and I handed her another pillow as she began to cry.

Patting her back, "Yes, Honey, now a new feeling is here. What feeling is it? Is it sad?"

She shakes her head in affirmation. "Yes, it is sad."

I pat her back, still following her process, and the sadness began to pass.

I handed her another pillow. "Do you remember what we do when our feelings are big?"

She said, "Belly Breathe."

"Yes, Sweetie, Belly Breathe with this pillow," as I stroked her back.

Then she begins to smile and giggle.

"I know this happens, Sweetheart. Now happiness is here, and it is funny."

"Meme, let's make a happy pillow!"

I take the last throw pillow from the day bed and draw a smiley face.

"Meme, let's make faces on all the pillows!"

Luckily, I was not attached to the pillows. They were recycled pillows from a resale store for my yoga practice and what was more important than this moment of learning with this precious child. So under her direction, I drew faces on each pillow: angry, sad, breathe, and smile. She wanted to try again. After a few cycles, she wanted to show her sister what she could do. This started the Feeling Circle practice that Avery would do each time she visited our farm to come current and cleanse her heart of her troubles in her life.

Our trying this strategy was spontaneous, and I followed my experience, love, and discernment with trust in the feelings and Avery's intuition. However, one could plan for a moment by having colored pillows for each feeling, or blank muslin pillows that child can make their own feeling pictures on or other soft items. As long as the items are made with a material that is soft and safe for throwing and hitting, and the child can relate to the item. Also, having an item allows for the identification of the feelings and some detachment of the intense emotions as they are placed outside of self for a path of feeling work that is followed each time. The elements support and track the circulation of the feelings from anger, sadness or hurt, breathing to calm down, and return to equilibrium. This brings clarity and order to the chaos of the interworld of grief and anger, not getting one's way and disappointment and for feeling hurt by actions in the world. I have found that a wave of anger that is not felt can turn inward and fester into self-harm that is heartbreaking to see in children and a cycle that needs interruption in a dynamic way. There are multiple ways to address anger in children, and this is one that is helpful for repeating anger that has hurt underneath; the anger from persistent situations of feeling helpless in a situation. While the situation may continue, a child can find self-modulation with their feelings and understanding of their feelings and not experience themselves as helpless as often.

I have witnessed my granddaughter gain pride through using her feeling pillows to the point of wanting to show her skills to everyone in her family. She is now teaching others how to do the Feeling Circle. She, on purpose, goes to her room in my home without slamming the door to release her feelings. I always check on her, breathe with her, and love her through the release of feelings.

Feeling Circle Process

In my work with therapists, I found a kinetic release of the unconscious feelings useful through pillow hitting. This strategy became well known in the '70s and was the source of jokes. However, I found after many years of talk therapy to add body to the investigation of what is holding me back or not expressed or what needs to be released as very helpful. With children who are still learning their full spectrum of feelings, expression, and choice around their feelings, this practice may bring forward their feelings in a safe manner with acceptance and protection. Doing this practice in a sequence teaches calming techniques for when feelings come up organically in everyday life. There is an order of common feeling expression.

Another advantage of holding space for a child to explore their feelings in this way allows the pressure cooker of feelings to be lessened while showing we have a choice in how we feel when we feel and expression of feeling as we mature and learn.

Some baseline conditions need to be in place before this practice is introduced. This is a therapeutic tool, so best done under those circumstances and guidance.

1. Have permission

If a family is seeing a therapist, that's perfect. I am writing this book for all loving adults in children's lives, and I know there are times when a family is not seeking therapy, or therapy is not available. I think loving and mature adults can hold space for children with the permission of the parents and child. The adult is responsible for themselves and the child, to be honest about their abilities, intent and have permission and support in all these tender moments with other human beings.

2. A developed and established trusting relationship

I have often written in this book about developing conn-ections and safety with children by listening to them and validating their experiences. Make sure you have a loving relationship of connection. Practice listening and inquiring with curiosity to show the child they matter. Be familiar and pay attention to their cues, and earn their trust in any therapeutic work you do together.

3. Set the environment

The context should have privacy. The child needs to know they will not be overheard or in trouble for their honest expression. Only adults with established relationships will hear and witness their moment of vulnerability and exploration. The environment should have soft textures, be safe from sharp corners and dangerous objects that the child may run into, fall into, or be poked or thrown. I prefer an open room with most furniture and objects removed or pushed out of the way. I like to have throw pillows, fluffy rugs, and soft blankets. Large back pillows for adults are useful as well. With younger children, I have pillows with feeling expressions drawn by a child: mad, sad, breathe, and calm. Sometimes, happiness and laughter come as well. Comfy stuffed animals and cloth dolls add to the comfort of the child and soft surroundings.

4. Choose the time

When a human is in chronic grief or trauma, there are so many moments to intervene. Choosing the moment to use this strategy is important. Make a plan, and set the environment and wait for the right circumstances to embark on this time of the feeling process. The adult is always in charge and holding the container and structure for the feeling child. Having patience and waiting for the moment when all elements support the intervention is best.

5. Amount of time

This is a very vulnerable process. Allocating time for rest and recovery is important. Make sure the child has as much time as they need for the expression and recovery before returning to social situations and demands.

Chapter

Twelve

Children Passing Their Skills On

The family was over to enjoy a multi-generational Thanksgiving gathering. I had spent a month planning the meal, decorations, setting the table, coordinating with the other adults to share in the dish prep, and special attention to everyone's favorite dishes. We had great grandparents traveling from another state, and our daughter was blending her fiancé and his two children into our family. I wanted to hostess a special holiday for us all appreciating us all together in peace.

We had a BIG snowstorm two days before Thanksgiving. The weather news reported it was the most snowfall in 24 hours. Luckily, I had been shopping for weeks, and when I was alone and snowed in on the farm for Tuesday and Wednesday, I had all I needed to get down to business for the making of Thanksgiving. It takes so much care and works to create the home for a stress-free holiday meal. This year, I wanted no drama, especially from me. I found love and nourishment from the luxury of time and energy to tend to those I care deeply for and an event I was looking forward to having.

I pulled my great grandmother's dishes from the top shelf to clean. I remembered sitting at the end of the meals at my mother's table with these dishes. I emptied the dining and living rooms to clean the floor, chipping beeswax and honey off the floor from our recent harvest without an ounce of resentment, which is unusual for me. I was feeling the appreciation that our family was in a place to gather in

119

love. Grateful for the snow to help me to buckle down and clean and prepare in such detail was a luxury. I appreciated NPR podcasts and time alone.

I had a tablecloth with ornamental hens and red and yellow designs I had picked up at a resale store on my last yoga retreat on the California Coast. Feeling excited to place the beeswax candles, fall flowers, and deep-colored platters on the table. As I set the table, I felt my female lineage, our appreciation for beauty, for serving our families as I laid the worn white china with silverware marks from meals past. Touching the dishes, I remembered the mashed potatoes from my preteen years in this serving dish. Holding the coffee cups, I remembered the first year I noticed the hot coffee smell and wondered and asked how they could drink coffee. The odor was distasteful to me. Today I looked forward to my husband, my daughter, and her partner, my dad, and his wife enjoying coffee from these cups. And now how this book relies on the delicious coffee.

To understand the depth of my appreciation for this opportunity for a loving holiday with family heirlooms and my full participation, I need to tell you some history. You see, since my mother's illness and death in the 1980s, there have been many chaotic times. I took on the family holidays at the age of 20. I was too young to have an appreciation of service. Or the experience of how to nurture myself or others through the process of planning for a holiday meal. All the drama-filled mistakes required to teach me what was important to me as the matriarch of a family have served their purpose. It has taken years to grow in that role and find peace and joy. I now know that all the consideration of the details and the pieces of love restore me. This planning was me taking Sacred Actions to heal my losses with endearment, honoring who and what I care about, and making work sacred. My sacred actions filled me full for Thanksgiving Day.

The table was beautiful. Something you should know, the children usually like to come and fight over who will sit where. Understanding the need for order, I was planning. I had placed cards in the shape of leaves that read I am grateful for _____. I wrote the name of each of the family members in the space on the placard. This time, I decided who sat where. The grandmother was in charge, and each of us was special. I was experiencing new growth for me to own as the matriarch. Boundaries created around the meal and safety of the children. Children feel safe when they know who is in charge.

Once I had the tables set, I began to worry which combo of children configuration would work best for the ease during dinner. After much consideration and talking with my daughter, I squeezed them all at the small table. I was setting a small table with bright, small plates and bowls with place cards and a centerpiece of pumpkins and gourds, which the children had permission to touch and move as they pleased.

Thanksgiving morning, the six-year-old came in and right away checked the table arrangements. I had missed a glass which she pointed out to me. Also, one chair was missing at the table. It was so funny to me how she had to assess the situation quickly. We remedied these two items, and she was able to relax and move on to play. I was so grateful for the first situation of possible stress that went smoothly.

We had a lovely visit and a meal. The children shared our fun blessing cheer to the new members of our family, including the children and great grandparents in a light and fun moment of praise to God. The littles ate without struggling. The food was varied and simple, making it pleasing to all. The children finished before the adults and were able to return to their activities, allowing the adults to continue to catch up with their visiting and story sharing. After a while, we spoke of the weekend plans. Some shuffling began between the two girls ending up with the same young granddaughter running to her room in my home. We heard some slamming in the room.

Giving her a few minutes, my daughter asked me if I would see what was upsetting her.

I knocked on the door and said, "Sweetie, I am coming in."

You may notice that I am repeating the way I had discovered supporting her on New Years' Eve the year before. She was hanging her head and slamming things around. I started inquiring. Avery began to pick up the pillows with faces drawn on them for our emotions practice. She hit the mad pillow. I moved out of the way and breathed.

After a few hits, I asked, "Are there words that go with your angry feelings?"

"No, not this time," she said.

She moved to the crying, sad pillow and then asked for the breathing pillow. The happy, laughing pillow was missing, so Avery asked me to draw a happy face on another pillow. I sat with her as she went through the feeling cycle a time or two. While holding the breath pillow, she was able to tell me what was upsetting her.

One of the little boys came to join us. He was curious about what Avery was doing.

I told him, "Avery is practicing expressing her feelings."

Avery got animated and said, "I'll show you. Say something 'mean' to me."

I smiled. Thomas gave me a doubtful look. Just like Avery had eleven months before. I nodded, "Yes, It's okay."

He said to Avery, "You are little."

She hit the pillow and said, "I'm mad."

Then she picked up the sad pillow and pretended to cry and said, "That hurts my feelings."

She continued through the sequence with a breathing pillow and a happy pillow. I felt astonished. Children are amazing. I was so proud of her teaching.

Continuing with her demonstration, she said, "I will say something mean, and you try."

He looked at me again and said, "Is this okay? Really?"

Loud and clear, I said, "It's okay, Honey. I am here."

She called him little. He hit the angry pillow. This little guy pushed the sad feeling pillow away and went to the breathe pillow and held on tight. Interesting. Avery handed him the happy pillow. I watched as they practiced one more time. By this time, his brother was checking in on the action. He was curious.

Avery told him, "We are practicing feelings. Do you want to try?"

"Avery, do you have this? Can I go back to the dining room?" I asked.

"Yup Meme. Come on, boys."

I went back to where the adults were visiting and allowed space for the kids to be kids and show, share, and practice with each other their emotional intelligence through play.

I found such humor and insight by watching these kids:

    Older to younger guidance

    What hurts them

    The power in acknowledging the hurt

The upfronts of saying something mean, right on the surface

The gentleness in Avery's teaching

I was a proud Meme!

"Love is an action verb." Author unknown

Chapter Thirteen

Discerning Intuition and Fear

Coronavirus: The importance of support when taking risks and learning to understand intuition and discerning fear.

When China was beginning to respond to the pandemic, my eldest daughter and I had been making plans for the last year to go to Southern India with her yoga teacher, which was an adventure for her and a dream come true for me. Some of our family members were concerned for us, so we did our research and listened to our connections to our Higher Powers and decided with precautions, it was safe and best for us to continue with our plans. Spoiler Alert: We returned unharmed, yet the world was changing before our eyes. We returned with increased resources to respond to the world as it shifted moment by moment.

The trip was enchanting. We rode our magic carpet into the future a day and back to reclaim that day without resistance. Several times before, I heard the call for a trip to foreign land and culture. The learnings that come from travels are unique and require leaving home, routines and comforts, going into the unknown, letting go of control, taking leaps and risks that affect yourself and your loved ones.

In 2005, I remembered the sheer panic I felt before my first time on a trip to the former Soviet Union. I thought for sure I was going to die and leave my daughters motherless like I was motherless at 18. I also felt it was my calling and duty to go for my growth, my service to others in a fantastic opportunity, and a request from my social worker community. My support group and teachers' problem solved my concerns and let me lean on their faith and experience that my fears meant something but maybe not what I thought they indicated. This new call required me to walk through the door of the unknown. To consider and discern what my intuition was telling me. Was this fear excitement as well? Are there real dangers to see? Am I safe? What precautions can I take to bring me safety and comfort? I got to work so I could walk into this breath-taking opportunity. I went into my list-making mode and "replacing mom" preps for my teenage daughters. I considered what I needed in my suitcase to keep me comfortable and well. I researched the customs, weather, money, and food I would encounter. I cried my deepest fears to the leaders of the group and leaped.

The trip was stunning, hard, and hooked me. I learned how to take risks on my behalf. I learned to investigate my fears and discern danger from the fear of the unknown or breaking social training from the culture of what good mothers do or don't do. In the unknown, I learned to build my reliance on my relationship to a Higher Power and listen and have faith. I learned to release my children a tiny bit to their own lives and other care providers. I was on the mighty wave, and it was messy. The surrender and sur-viving were life-changing. The delightful meeting like-hearted people around the world brought laughing, sharing, crying, and loving the embrace of sameness in women no matter where they live expanded my aspirations. My worldview grew so large that I only knew a little. I wanted to have friends from everywhere.

I did come to some hardships. There were difficulties with the trip. For instance, I cried so hard I wet myself in a van on a dirt road far from what I knew. One night my daughter so missed me, and I worried and missed her and being out of cell range; I only knew she was trying to reach me, and the call would not stay connected. She tried some new dangerous behaviors that night with painful results. I developed diarrhea and sleeplessness. And still, the rewards were vast and fruitful. It was all part of this international world soup of opportunities.

Today, I am grateful I took these risks before providing experience with assessing concerns with travel at the beginning of coronavirus. To show my daughter a deeper faith, to witness her maturing to the next stage, and opening to her roots of wisdom within herself, I could support and know we are okay. We were okay if we went, we were okay if we stayed home, we could change our minds in a moment when real evidence (not FEAR: false evidence appearing real) of concern crossed our paths. My daughter and I shared a deep integration of our bond and faith. We will always know it was for us during one, short two-week time in February 2020. She walked into the Chicago airport with a supported experience in trusting her gut and taking risks on her behalf. Initiating me into being the mother of an adult woman sharing life, adventure, and dreams. I sit in wonder and gratitude for the fortuity of parenthood.

As I write this, the virus still has much to teach us and is not over and harming many. I want my words to tend to the parents and children, teachers and leaders, grandparents, aunts, and uncles to be there for the children who are losing and grieving. I want to rearrange and respond to my paradigm shift about loss. Since my friend's death in such an honorable way that included everyone, a space to feel and participate, and my daughter and I taking risks in our best interest, my paradigm of fear and grief is changing. I have a palpable sensation of the ground below me and the sky above. I am not in charge and do not always know best. That Mother Earth is responding to humans, and we are one. We are all interconnected and have enough when we share. I feel peace in a way that I would not expect a pandemic to produce in me. Like the world is slowing down and paying attention in a collective exhale. The exhalation feels relaxing to me. The collective feels full to me. Like the scream, I have heard since the early 2000s as a mother and teacher. Maybe the scream I have wanted to scream since my childhood screamed, "STOP, Listen, love, and respond."

Chapter
Fourteen

Expectation Story

Expectations and the Coronavirus

As we were adjusting to not knowing daily, when people would stop getting sick, I began to notice how I was coping with this unknown by creating new expectations, for the unique situation, new ways to be comfortable in chaos. I noticed I was not alone in the strategy for comfort. The children and the animals were doing the same. Each time we had new restrictions in our environment, the disappointments would come and be solved by creating new expectations. Anytime the new solution to the limit created an expectation, and when that solution did not work, the disappointment would return. The human condition of wanting consistency, predictability, calm during inconsistency was intense and solved by creating expectations of predictability.

Yes, we are human beings. We can be reliable but not consistent like the sun. Up to this point in time, the sun has risen daily. Humans are not like the sun, though, as I try. As a caring, loving human being, I try to be consistent with my loved ones. I try to have that kind of consistency in my life, but "the law of life is change." I am a human being, so this takes me back to my story about Jacob. I was building trust with Jacob that I would be there for him, and the way I was doing that was in creating expectations. I would show up each morning with a snack on the playground, and when I saw him on Monday, Tuesday, and Wednesday, he was relaxing. I would do so on Thursday. Where does Jacob's mind go with his meanings and feelings if I don't show up on Friday? He expects that I will bring him a snack, and he will see me, have a hug, and feel safe or cared for, and I am there for him. Human beings are the ones who make expectations. I wanted to build trust with him. I did my best to be consistent. He wanted to feel safe and loved, and he came to rely upon me that I would be there for him. We joined in creating an expectation on purpose to build trust and change the previous expectations of "nobody cares about me or is here for me."

We create expectations ourselves, for each other and within ourselves. Since we create them, we can change them, and at some point, as humans will not be able to rise and set like the sun, we will be inconsistent and experience unmet expectations. At some point, the change will occur because it always does. That is a fundamental law. We will need to change the expectation that we created. Since we constructed it, we can change it. We may outgrow our expectations. The expectation may not fit for us anymore.

People learn how to handle disappointment when our expectations and reality differ. Adjusting unmet expect-ations was demanding work for my little fellow, Jacob. He had expected his mother to tend to his needs and life. He expected his father to show up for him during his fear and sadness. He had expectations of how his teachers would treat him and expected to have friends to keep him company. He assumed he would be able to write quickly. In addition to building new expectations in him that someone could be trustworthy, I was hoping to shift his internal expectations of himself to his internal expectations of the human condition of life in general, like I had to as I healed from my mother's death. If I did not arrive one morning, he had an unmet expectation. Building trust incorporates creating expectations. Trust is something we do and learn. Therefore, we can change and be in charge of expectations. My teachers taught me that the human condition gives us opportunities to consider, cope, and survive how we show up and how we cope with matters. If we accept the situation as it is, and take risks on our behalf, live on life's terms, we heal ourselves. Being in charge of our own experiences brings choices, empowerment, and peace. We can rise like the sun to the opportunities.

While I am deeply pained by so much suffering and loss during the coronavirus outbreak, this is not the first time the human race has faced and had human suffering at this level. Our species grows from how we cope. The question is, how are we going to cope with the new realities facing us. The expectations are changing, and our lifestyles are changing, revelations and new insights are happening all around us right now. During this occasion, we can build resiliency. This coronavirus is giving us a collective body experience.

"Life is not the way it is supposed to be. It is the way it is. The way you cope with it is what makes the difference."
Virginia Satir

Chapter

Fifteen

Necessity: The Mother of all Inventions

The increased use of technology for human connections, where at one time it would take months to leave your homeland and go to another continent to be able to connect with new people, brings us together. Today you can turn on your phone or a computer and very quickly see the face of a friend on another continent. We can see the face of a friend in another location holding a play session on the floor with a two-year-old and his mom.

While we are in quarantine, the ability to accept what our expectations are and shift to a new set of expectations allowed for the creative life force to come through us. And problem solves addressing the sincerest hope to connect during quarantine takes us deeper into the power of human flexibility. We find a way because that deep yearning is so potent and durable that the social distancing does not stop the human connection. Stay at home orders do not stop that a two-year-old is still growing and learning. Learning social skills is enhanced by spending time with other people outside of a two-year-old's immediate family.

His creative mother puts the computer on the floor while he is playing with his blocks and tells him, "There is Michelle. Say 'Hi' to Michelle."

He looks at the video and says, "Hi, Michelle."

I said, "Hi!" back and asked, "What are you doing, A?"

We model for our children the elasticity to be able to adjust to the circumstances as they are.

"I am building with my blue blocks," A responded.

"Your blue block," I repeat back to him.

"How many blue blocks do you have?"

His mother picks up each blue block and counts out loud for him, and adds, "A, you have three blue blocks."

He says, "Three."

To help... To improve... To create... To innovate...

I am so touched by the resilience, the creative abilities of the human spirit, and intellectual trust. Trust is an action, and expectations are actions. We use the coping of acceptance; accepting life on life's terms, we model the elasticity to be able to do so we actively teach the fluidness of change. The ability to change our inner world to the effect of the outer world. Our ability to receive the external world as it is. From there, we can problem solve and shift our internal role in our external world.

"I believe the greatest gift I can conceive of having from anyone is to be seen by them, heard by them, to be understood and touched by them." Virginia Satir

Chapter

Sixteen

Spring Renewal During Coronavirus

Children, are you enjoying time at home with your families? Time to roam and ask questions, to wander and wonder, participate around the house, and do activities with your parents more, sleep, and eat when you need? Are you trying old fashion activities your parents and grandparents remember?

Meme remembers climbing trees like you to see what I could see. It felt so good to climb and climb and test my abilities. Then once I was up high, I sat and looked at the blue of the sky—the breeze when slow felt like a hug. When the wind blew strong, I held on and felt brave. On a gentle day, I would rest and feel calm. Sometimes I took a book with me and read while laying on a branch. My brother and sister would leave me alone. I felt grown up away from my mother. The solace was new in a certain way for me. I was excited to be close to the clouds and watch them dance through the sky. To find peacefulness, the freedom to be alone and hear the sounds around me and see far felt so good. I still sense it now.

One of the silver linings of schools being closed for our family was more time for the children on our farm. I love creating a supportive environment for children to explore their interests in the natural world. When our nine-year-old granddaughter began climbing her tree multiple times a day at her mother's house, then visited the farm and climbed the tree in the front yard on our farm, this memory resurfaced for me. And with the recollection of my childhood tree climbing, one of my base beliefs about learning in children needed attention in this book. I find nature can provide real nourishment for us all and is part of the mandala. Given the space to be curious and risk-taking humans, many children will attempt physical challenges to broaden their boundaries as well as test their physical and emotional limits. Through these activities, children gain self-knowledge and personal coping strategies. Many of these strategies are very healthy. So much of what I experienced up in the cherry tree in front of my parents' home while I was in the second grade I carry today on to my yoga mat and practice. I see this happening with my granddaughter on the soccer field and up the tree. She took her bug catcher box and scissors to the hang from the tree, so she had her tools for capturing her discoveries like I have my journal.

It gratified me that this nine-year child has the space to explore as a child as the expectations of growing up, and she feels the changes in her body. She is beginning the transition between young childhood towards the older child to teen that, with some sadness of not wanting to leave behind the innocence, she sees her siblings still have, and she is losing. We, too, feel concerned and sad about her leaving childhood and the possibility of losing some of her intactness. She has a healthy self and her abilities up to this point in her life. Can we add and support her through this transition and help her maintain herself through the double digits of life? We hope so. I do know that her connection to nature and her wild curiosity is one way to support her transition.

Chapter

Seventeen

Yoga Practice for Children

"I am Happy"

Another day during quarantine, I visited my daughter's home. I had only seen the family once in six weeks. Being the hands-on grandmother I am, this was unusual, yet we are living in exceptional times. The six-year granddaughter and I mainly wanted to connect and feel each other this day. She was talkative and inviting with me, showing me her unicorn headband and purse. Unicorns were her new spirit animal. She wanted everything unicorn. Unicorns being her favorite, she had started around the new year and now was in full passion mode. I smiled and smiled at her beauty and love of all things unicorn. There is a way she is so like her mother that brings me such joy.

We had school time for all four children this day. Mommy and I organized the lesson plans that the teachers so generously brought to the footsteps of each child's home. Absolutely, a shout out to the fantastic teachers during coronavirus! Popi was to take two of the children to recess while I sat with the two of the children doing a few assignments. The kids were excited about a familiar structure and also to show to their siblings and me their knowledge. I had it more uncomplicated than a class of 30 students or a mother of four. The older siblings enjoyed helping, and the younger enjoyed the attention of their prized older sisters. Then it was lunchtime, and we were all still enjoying our pretend school day.

After lunch: free time. Awe, free time. It was one of those beautiful, sunny, spring days we have in Colorado that is so warm that I doubt it will ever be cold again and summer is here. The bikes are out, and everyone is showing me their tricks I had missed in recent months. They have gained so much speed and skills on their bikes. The oldest socialized with her cul de sac friends.

Here is what I am leading up to. Avery saw me sitting in the grass crossed legged. She came up to me and quietly took my hands and laid them on my knees and placed my fingers in the meditation pose. Several years of sharing my practice of yoga and meditation with the children and Avery saw and felt the moment. She asked if she could take my cell phone to the porch. Avery turned on a yoga song we have played and practiced in the past, "I Am Happy" by Snatam Kaur, and started her gentle movement. Gradually, she sat in the hero pose and added the arm movements that she had learned that go with this song. She saw me watching her now, so we made the gestures together and smiled.

A year before this moment, a yoga friend of mine, Rachel Zelaya, offered a class for little girls. One Sunday morning, five little girls, a mother and I met in the studio. Rachel led in a circle through asanas named after animals, songs, and sharing. One of the songs was, "I Am Happy" by Snatam Kaur. The teacher taught the movements that go with the lyrics. My heart and face filled with the biggest smile ever.

My little girl inside was so happy. My tendency towards sadness lifted. The girls giggled. With each round of the song, we got more pleased. Our happiness grew and grew. The depth of what we were singing rang in my soul. How pure was this?! At the end of class, the teacher asked which part of the 45 minute class was our favorite.

I said, "I Am Happy!"

My granddaughter said, "'I Am Happy' is my favorite too!"

I added this song and its movements to my daily practice. I noticed, I rose from my yoga mat singing and smiling through the day when I practiced this song on my mat. I began to sing the song with the grandkids, every once in awhile, when we were hanging out. They asked me to play the song on my cell phone. Spontaneously, we would kneel and practice the moves. Sometimes, I noticed a funk fill the air around me or us, and I called upon the practice and sang to myself to raise my vibration. I can know sadness. We can allow grief. Also, I recognize when this moment is not a grief moment. It is a moment to be alive, and I sing "I Am Happy."

Another time, about nine months ago, we took all four kids to the Denver Zoo. There were many fruitions of sacred actions that day. But to stay with the storyline here, following the day at the zoo, in the tired car ride home, the children began fighting and getting out of hand and making it hard to focus on the road. I put this song "I Am Happy" on the car stereo and began practicing yoga for myself, primarily to keep me calm and patient, and to shift the energy and hoping the kids would join in while Popi drove. Maybe you remember the "If You Are Happy and You Know It" song from preschool? Same idea. Soon the girls did join and stopped picking on each other, and then the boys, while new to this song and movement, were curious and joined—a little reprieve. We teach and practice during the calm to have tools during the storm.

Addyson helped me plan a yoga lesson for her kindergarten class in 2015. The teacher and children loved learning yoga.

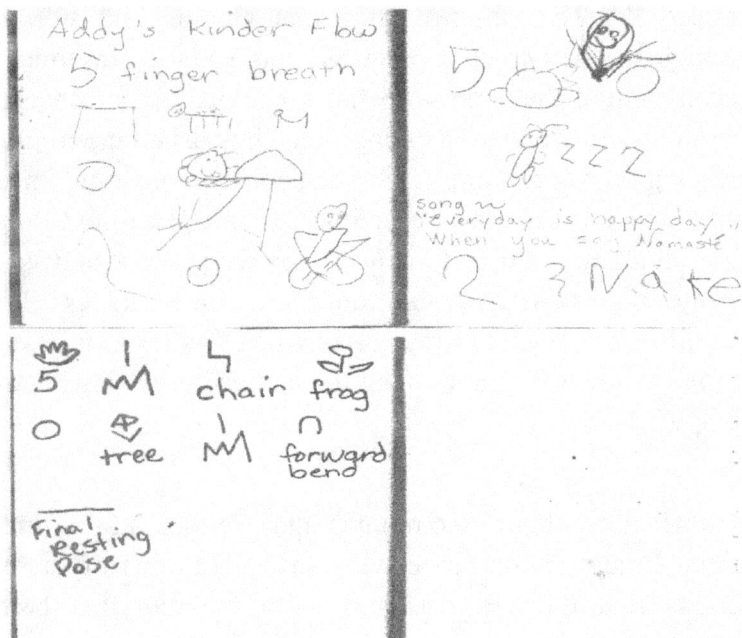

Chapter

Eighteen

Mother's Day Gardening as Sacred Action

So often, I felt adrift losing my mother on the cusp of womanhood, struggling with traditions and rituals, and just how to live life as an adult. I have spoken in this book about my discovery and use of these highly charged moments as opportunities to grow and establish my creativity. The empowerment I feel in finding ways to honor my feelings of loss enhanced by remembering the impact of the relationship with a loved one who has passed and feeling their place, connection, and gifts in my life than to do more than get through the feelings of these moments.

One of these moments is Mother's Day. When my children were young, I still did not know how to honor my feelings and just got through the day. I would be sad all week and barely function on the Sunday of Mother's Day with a pretend smile on my face. Once I became a single mother, I could not hide. The kids had eagle eyes with their security at stake. The children motivated me to learn ways to tend to myself and life better for their sake.

In Colorado, the wives' tale is, it is frost safe to plant gardens starting the Sunday of Mother's Day. While this is changing as the climate changes, if I choose the flowers and plants wisely with pansies and other cool temperature tolerant flowers and the greens of spinach, kale, and lettuces, I can enjoy planting on this day. I established the tradition of waiting to plant flower containers until

Mother's Day. The waiting is part of the honoring. I allow myself to feel my mother and notice the flowers and colors that are calling me. I sense what colors bring me joy. I look in magazines for new arrangements and combinations I like, and flowers my mother may have admired. I build anticipation instead of dread. I give myself power instead of abandonment. I respect that my mother was a woman with her struggles and raised me to be the woman I am in love with. We share strength and wounds, and I can celebrate spring and our power. Choosing to connect with the deep mother, Mother Earth, that way, my mother and I are both held. I grow spiritually and emotionally. That is what sacred actions offer. Planting flowers on a day set aside for mothers, I belong to the collective society and am not alone. Self-pity is not viable at that moment under these conditions. Reversing self-pity was the lesson I carried for Jacob, Joseph, and all the ones not named here. First, I learned this lesson for myself before I could share the experience. We help children with grief this way.

Last year, I planned long and worked harder on my Mother's Day Garden. There was an area that had been covered by a ramp to our front porch for the previous owners. As they had aged, they built a wooden ramp over the cement stairs and part of a dirt area. The ramp was decaying and becoming unsafe. Midwinter, we removed the ramp and exposed a small area of dirt without grass or rocks. Living in Boulder, Colorado, this is a gardener's dream; established dirt without stones and rocks. We are named Boulder for a reason. I saw the opportunity. Smiling to myself, I saw my Mother's Day project. The second week in May, I began turning the dirt and adding more rich planting dirt. The nursery was displaying deep purple and white pansies with golden dot centers. Our Craftsman-style house completed in 1946 is on five acres of land. I had tried to keep to a white farmhouse decor with some touches of Art & Craftsman Style. Selecting flowers in threes, three colors, three types, annuals, and a white ground cover, I made a feminine, sweet Mother's Garden that made me smile daily. I also felt my resilience to keep myself open to love and to be alive, as seen in this garden. I did the work myself and planted each flower with prayer and care, just like the ribbons on my first Christmas tree as a single woman.

Grief can take us down. It is not a small feat when we learn to live with disappointment, fear, loss, and anger. We can grow and change. If we grew up in unsafe situations, we can create safe zones in our futures. Our children will take on that task as adults. In our schools, we have specific dangers and challenges with pandemics and gun violence that this generation faces. It will be no small feat for us to show up for the children and ourselves and advance our society and maintain our humanness and connections with positive, caring actions.

I do not think we need another task force, committee, or pharmaceutical drug to heal and show up for our children right now. We need to get a hold of our humanness and listen to our children. To care for our children and be strong in faith and character. Fearless in the hard things. I am proud when I show up for myself in sacred actions and share myself with a child.

"Compassion begins with the capacity to hold your own life with a loving heart. Whenever you're aware that you are suffering, if you offer yourself through attention, words and touch-compassion will naturally awaken."
Tara Brach, PH.D.

Chapter
Nineteen

Loss in Current Times

Practice and Resiliency

It was a Sunday morning several months into the pandemic. This cloudy day started with my husband telling me I needed to come to look. "There's been a disaster outside." A bear had entered on our property and tore the chicken wire off the coop in the backyard, where my "cheer me up during quarantine" silkie chicks lived. Remnants of their feathers laid on the ground. It had been a hard week with a dear friend in my life being in and out of the hospital with heart surgery, in addition to the cultural tragedy of a pandemic. I got dressed and went outside without doing my meditation and yoga practice. I watered the seedlings in the front yard, watched the dog in his morning grass pee, and picked up the compost bins and the flower pot from my front yard table that the bear had knocked over.

Facing the effortless first, then going to the coop, I collected the blood-stained silkies' feathers before the children visited and saw the evidence of the destruction. Tolku was staying close to me. A beautiful characteristic of Lhasa Apsos' is that they keep track of their people rather than a person keeping track of the dogs. It is his job to stay a few steps behind me. This week I was his substitute person, while his primary person recovered from surgery, and he remained safe on the farm. We walked out to the horses. They were out in the field. Typically when I come to the corral, they meet me right away. As soon as I open the back door each morning, they come to the corral gate, waiting for shoulder scratches and breakfast. Not this morning. I collected their bowls, which have been licked clean, unlike how the horses leave them. As I write, it occurred to me; I would pause in the future when I put food out for the horses after a bear visit.

While I noticed and confirmed that the bear had been in the horse area last night, it did not have meaning to me. I am still learning. I picked up the bowls and poured the senior feed, beet flakes, and garlic, mixed it up, and placed it in the manger of the corral. Very unusual that horses still had not come in close to the feeding area. As I said their names, Coco, the mare, moved a little faster towards me. She just loves and needs her morning feed. Ranger, the gelding, cautiously looked over to the left of the field at the tree border that surrounds as a natural habitat around the orchard. That's when I realized they were very cautious and scared, and maybe the bear was still nearby. Maybe Ranger can even see the bear, probably at least smell it. I did not. I considered picking up the feed so as not to attract the bear. I didn't think that would help, so I stood to watch for a few minutes, building some confidence that Ranger had the situation under control better than I would. Reasoning with myself it would be better if I left the barn, I went to my car with Tolku and opened the door and pushed on the car horn. Blaring the horn to warn the bear and let off a little steam myself. I was mad at that bear and had illusions of telling him with the horn, "I will not stand for this destruction. Stay away from my animals and me." I felt a little better honking the horn at the bear.

I was so upset to have optimistically and naively thought the chickens were safe again. This was the third year we had an early freeze in the spring, causing the food to be sparse in the foothills. This was the earliest in the season that a bear had shown up on our property. I wasn't prepared for the bear season already. Luckily, the hive yards all had electric fencing around them. "Do we have to freakin' surround the farm with electric fencing the whole property!" Electric fencing around the whole of the property is just a fantasy. I felt so much anger, frustration, and guilt that I hadn't been able to protect my babies. The babies I raised to cheer me up during quarantine. They had become so cute, and I could watch them scurry through the chicken run. I had hopes that the silkies would mother other babies in the future.

"Don't count your chickens before they hatched."

I came into the house feeling scratchy at my husband. Being tempted to blame him, yet I knew better. I thought, "Should I eat breakfast or start over with yoga and meditation time?" I opened the fridge. Something was so stinky in there. I cleaned that out, and Dean said he was going to make an omelet, and I asked him to make some for me too. Thank you, goodness! I don't want to pick a fight with my husband. I am going to my room where I have my sheepskin rug.

"Thank you, Honey, and I'm going to my meditation room while you make breakfast. Okay?" I said and asked.

"Sure," he replied.

Tears pressed right behind my eyes, wanting to shed. They were stuck and dry. To my yoga space, I go. Not my grieving tent in the coop due to the weather and all. I lit one of my beeswax candles and burned some palo santo wood. The incense was helping. It's a cleansing wood, and sometimes the smell of it kind of repels me, but this morning it was such a pleasant, luscious smell for me.

I turned over one of my inspiration cards, and it read: "Life supports you. You are safe." I will take that. I go to my music and play the children's blessing yoga album, "Feeling Good Today" by Snatam Kaur. Feeling a metaphoric hand on my back of support from the music and lighting another sweet incense strip, I laid my back on the floor with my mat, blanket, and furry skin below me. I took off my glasses and started raising my legs up and down one at a time, exercising my morning navel exercises while stretching my hamstrings and spine, my breath increases and water bubbles to the surface and out my eyes. With tears releasing from my eyes, sadness felt. I am tenderizing.

My muscles in my body and my energy around me were supportive and full. "I loved those chickens. I miss them. I'm tired of being so resilient during this hard time. And meanwhile, I am held." It felt good to release the tears finally. With the feeling on the fur below me and hearing the music, I moved to my morning bridge pose, lifting and dropping my hips and spine, allowing the psoas to open my front surface and extend my spine. The morning exercises that my body told me over a year ago, I needed each day. I have been practicing regularly though this year of writing this book. I say to myself, "I can receive support." Then I hear my husband's phone ring. I started doing the bicycle pedaling exercise and sacred tantrum surfaces.

"*#@*, painful anger!" I yell in my mind.

Now the physical and muscular pain that comes through holding anger and fear surfaced. I have been practicing every day. There's still just so much freaking loss and grief to process, to feel.

The sacred tantrum doesn't last long. It was quieter, given that I am in my house—an example of why the griefing tent was outside for privacy. I will need to go to the grieving tent later to let the loud out, but now I want to be comfortable here and as raindrops start spitting on my window through the cloudy sky. Mother Earth has water needs. The tears from the sky and me return to the Earth. Internally, I continued to be frustrated for a few moments. Today was a day to soften and allow the moisture to moisten me during the dry times. To moisten the earth so that we can all grow. The seedlings, I remember the flowers. A moment of gratitude for the movement of tears, the water of tears though the exhale as I brought my feet to earth. I bent my knees toward the sky and placed my hands on my belly, Belly Breathing deeply. Moving one hand to my chest, the three-part breath I have practiced so many times with my teachers and taught with other women.

"Yes, God is here. I need to be doing this. All I can do is my piece. It is best not to be spiraling out of control, wanting to control the outcome. My job right now was to align with what is true and the Higher Power. I cannot control what happened last night." I still want to change how we live in co-existence with this bear. It has been five years now that bears have been visiting at night. I am tired and allow myself to be tired by myself to feel the breath and continue breathing.

I rise to my knees, and the "I am Happy" song comes on, so I move into the mudras and movements with that song. I do not feel happy, but I know I am breathing deeper. I am alive, and it's my job right now to breathe and be alive while there is death going on around me. It is not my time to die, not my time to hold my breath, so I do the movements. I practice with the support of the music. I moved into my twisted open heart series on my knees. After twisting, I sit on my sit bones and straddle my legs for the life nerve stretch. I was stretching the back of my legs, increasing my breath speed, and lengthening my spine. Sometimes moving, sometimes pausing for a long stretch of the muscles, feeling the deep. Then I shift into dropping my chest and heart towards the floor, having a devotion to Mother Earth and all that breathes me.

Bringing my legs into a butterfly pose, "Ouch, Ouch, I have so much pain in my right hip." It has not been right since a car accident several years ago. I breathed into my hip, reached forward, and rocked my legs, bringing circulation to my joints. "Oh, the pain in my right hip, listen. Yes, this is the work, being with the grief, being with the pain, and listening. Greasing the joint, moving it, not letting it take me down." Then, I begin to butterfly my legs some more.

"Ooooh, that feels good, greasing the internal oil in my joints." It was time to stand and bring my hands to my chest. I pause. Bow. Next, dropping arms to my sides for mountain pose. I brought the bolster close to my feet and began squatting and rising to a gentle forward bend, squat, stand, squat, stand. Building my heart rate opens all parts of my body, building strength and flexibility in the heart. The heart is open while I squatted and exhaled. Straight legs, I forward bend, inhaled up and down 26 times.

I felt proud of myself when I finished 26 cycles, because I wanted to stop at six but asked for help and remembered other times I wanted to stop and didn't and felt better. "I have built resiliency through the hardest parts. I got on my mat today. I made a decision and made each step towards success; I cared for myself. Each step has been pure discipline and devotion to say yes to my own best health and interest." I am feeling relief, as well. I am feeling better. I am near the end, so I stand up straight with my arms down by my side and follow my breath.

I was doing my side stretches, the homestretch, the easy-peasy sections of my asana practice. After several side sketches, I place one hand on my heart and extend the other behind me. Beginning with an inhale extending my arm from my heart and exhaling my left arm to twist behind me, opening my heart through the front side and back side of my torso. During one expulsion of breath, I begin to swing a little bit and have some playfulness in me. I remember, "Oh yes, my pain always takes me back to the original wound and coping I learned in my childhood. It's my little girl. She hurts today. I am changing the way my little girl learned to cope with pain and sadness." I went through the cycle today. "Oh, the musing and the magic of this book. About the process that I have pieced together from my teachers and personalized for myself. I was bringing myself back to walking my talk. I am healing her each day with discipline, allowing myself to be exposed and authentic. The devotion to myself into what breathes my breath. I feel happy in a little giddy girl way."

Now I am ready. I want to connect with one of the special helpers in my life. I started thinking about them. "Yeah, I need support now. I got through it today, very well, but it was a trudge through the mud. I don't want to rely on my bucket without filling it high for all the needs of resilience tested right now. The sensing work worked." I bring my arms out perpendicular to my body. And begin the inhale and exhale of opening my neck and throat to be able to speak. Open my voice to ask for help and share my story, and to be available to my loved ones. I circled my head and neck. The prana energy rose from the Earth through me to above my head. I pick up my phone to dictate this story, while I still have courage and awareness and clarity. Thank you, dear dictation app. Thank you, book. Thank you, little girl. Thank you, thank you for all the beauty that supports me sensing feelings and keeping my body healthy so that I can experience life and loss, so that I can remain open. Do more than surviving the "effing" losses. May adults pick up these gifts and start to train children younger to thrive and love themselves through loss.

"I experience all people being capable of change."
Virginia Satir

In Closing

I do not think it is an accident that many of my stories from my own family at this time are from holidays. One, I am a grandparent, and that is when we spend time together. Two, holidays are ripe with stress, and expectations met and unmet, leading to opportunities for feeling work, for grief to visit or revisit. I have done a lot of my own personal work around accepting my mother being absent from my holidays and in my life with my children and grandchildren. This is where my experience lives, and I suspect I am not alone in this experience.

Now, the coronavirus is where the rubber meets the road. The pandemic has created many unmet expectations, unknowns, and losses. We are in a cultural moment of grief, and I hope my experiences may serve many children and families.

I started writing this book from a nudge from my Higher Power. As I accepted the call and committed to follow and listen to the voice inside that spoke after the day my daughter and grandchildren came to me for love with such a big loss in their lives saying, "Share this story. This is the purpose of how your life has unfolded with a loss so young." Sacred Pictures, Avery's Story and Farm, Drums, and Animals were the first two stories to come to the page. This book is the prayerful vehicle of description and organization of how I live, grow, and guide through grief, and may those in need be served by my experiences.

I have read all of these books repeatedly with children. They are listed with younger children in mind for older children.

Book Recommendations:

Younger Children

Al-Ghani, K.I. and Al-Ghani, Haitham (2009). *The Red Beast Controlling Anger In Children With Asperger's Syndrome*. Jessica Kingsley Publishers.

Andersen, Hans Christian. *Ugly Duckling*.

Aragon, Jane Chelsea (1989). *Salt Hands*. E.P. Dutton, New York, N.Y. A Division of NAL Penguin Inc.

Barnwell, Ysaye M. and Saint James, Synthia (1998). *No Mirrors In My Nana's House*. Harcourt Brace and Company.

Berry, Joy (1996). *Let's Talk About Book Series: Feeling Sad*. Scholastic Inc.

Brandenberg, Aliki (1984). *Feelings*. Scholastic Inc.

Bright, Rachel (2012). *Love Monster*. Farrar Straus Giroux.

Frankel, Alona (1990). *I Want My Mother*. Israel; HarperFestival A Division HarperCollins Publishers.

Frankel, Alona (1996). *On Grandparents' Farm*. Israel; HarperFestival A Division HarperCollins Publishers.

Gates, Mariam and Hinder, Sarah Jane (2016). *Good Morning Yoga A Pose-By-Pose Wake-Up Story*. Sounds True, Inc.

Gilman, Phoebe (1992). *Something From Nothing*. Scholastic Inc.

Henkes, Kevin (1991). *Chrysanthemum*. A Mulberry Paperback Book.

John, Jory and Oswald, Pete (2019). *The Good Egg*. HarperCollins Children's Books, a division of HarperCollins Publishers.

Kavan, Stefan and Barbara and Otis, Michaelin (2011). *Trainman Gaining Acceptance And Friends Through Special Interests*. AAPC Publishing.

Lang, Suzanne and Lang, Max (2018). *Grumpy Monkey*. Random HouseChildren's Books, a division of Penguin House LLC, New York.

Most, Bernard (1990). *The Cow That Went Oink*. Scholastic, Inc.

Mayer, Mercer (2013). *Just A Big Storm*. HarperFestival, an imprint of HarperCollins Publishers.

Mayer, Mercer (1985). *Just Grandpa and Me*. Random House.

Morris, Ann(1995). *Shoes, Shoes, Shoes*. Lothrop, Lee & Shepard Books.

Munsch, Robert and Martchenko, Michael (1945). *Stephanie's Ponytail*. Annick Press Ltd.

Lobe, Arnold (1970). *Frog And Toad Are Friends*. Scholastics, Inc. by arrangement with Harper & Row, Publishers, Inc.

Oxenbury, Helen (1988). *Tom And Pippo Make A Mess*. Discovery Toys and Walker Books, Ltd.

Schartz, Amy (1988). *Annabelle Swift, Kindergartner*. Orchard Books, A Division of Franklin Watts, Inc.

Scott King, Coretta and Bryan, Ashley (2007). *Let It Shine Three Favorite Spirituals*. Atheneum Books for Young

Readers. An Imprint of Simon and Schuster Children's Publishing Division.

Sendak, Maurice (1963). *Where The Wild Things Are.* Harper and Row.

Tillman, Nancy (2005). *On The Night You Were Born.* Feiwel and Friends, an imprint of Macmillan.

Williams, Sue and Vivas, Julie (1998). *Let's Go Visiting.* Harcourt Brace & Company.

*Wood, Audrey and Wood, Don (1987). *Heckedy Peg.* Harcourt Brace Jovanovich, Publishers.

Wood, Audrey and Wood, Don (1982). *Quick As A Cricket.* Child's Play (International) Ltd.

Yorinks, Arthur and Egielski, Richard (1986). *Hey, Al.* Collins Publishers, Toronto.

Intermediate Elementary

Babbitt, Natalie (1975). *Tuck Everlasting.* Farrar, Straus and Giroux.

Blume, Judy (1972). *Tales Of A Fourth Grade Nothing.* Dutton

Clements, Andrew and Selznick, Brain (1996). *Frindle.* Simon & Schuster Books for Young Readers.

Curtis, Chirstopher Paul (1999). *Bud, Not Buddy.* Delacorte Books.

DiCamilla, Kate (2000). *Because Of Winn-Dixie.* Candlewick Press.

Gantos, Jack (2000). *Joey Pigza Loses Control.* HarperTrophy, A Division of HarperCollinsPublishers.

Hesse, Karen (1996). *The Music Of Dolphins*. Scholastic, Inc.

Naylor, Phyllis Reynolds (1991). *Shiloh*. Atheneum.

Paulsen, Gary (1986). *Hatchet*. MacMillan.

Polacco, Patricia (2010). *Junkyard Wonders*. Philomel Books, a division of Penguin Young Readers Group.

Polacco, Patricia (1988). *Thank You, Mr. Falker*. Philomel Books, a division of Penguin Young Readers Group.

Ryan, Pam Munoz (2000). *Esperanza Rising*. Scholastic.

Sachar, Louis (1998). *Holes*. Farrar, Straus and Giroux.

Williams, Garth (1952). *Charlotte's Web*. HarperTrophy, A Division of HarperCollinsPublishers.

References:

Brach, Tara (2003). *Radical Acceptance Embracing Your Life With The Heart Of A Buddha*. New York, New York. Bantam Books, A Division of Random House, INC.

Satir, Virginia (1988). *The New Peoplemaking*. Mountain View, Ca. Science and Behavior Books, Inc.

https://creducation.net

https://cresst.org.uk

Music Recommendations:

Snatam Kaur. "I am Happy." Feeling Good Today, Spirit Voyage Records. 2008.

Snatam Kaur. Feeling Good Today, Spirit Voyage Records. 2008.

About The Author

Michelle Ryan is a mother, grandmother, retired school teacher with her master of arts degree from CU Boulder in MultiCultural and Social Diversity Education specializing in Special Education and English as a Second Language. She has traveled with several nonprofits to Central Asia supporting people to people connections and self esteem work. Michelle has thirty years experience volunteering on the boards of three humanitarian organizations. She has facilitated women's retreats and loves being with women. She currently lives with her husband, a beekeeper, on a farm in Boulder County and spends her time listening to the Universe and creating.

www.ingramcontent.com/pod-product-compliance
Lightning Source LLC
LaVergne TN
LVHW020929090426
835512LV00020B/3277